COOL THINGS HAPPEN WHEN YOU SPEAK A FOREIGN LANGUAGE

COOL THINGS HAPPEN WHEN YOU SPEAK A FOREIGN LANGUAGE

WILLIAM B. GALLAGHER, MD

AND

CHRISTOPHER J. GALLAGHER, MD

Willowgate Press
East Setauket, NY

COOL THINGS HAPPEN WHEN YOU
SPEAK A FOREIGN LANGUAGE

Willowgate Press
Box 86
248 Route 25A
East Setauket, NY 11733
http://www.willowgatepress.com
author's website: christophergallagher.com

Printed in the United States of America

ISBN: 978-1-930008-08-3

Dedication

To the foreman on duty when the Tower of Babel came crashing down. I wonder what language he swore in?

Contents

Introduction

"The purpose of all knowledge is to impress people at cocktail parties."

Kim Gallagher, PhD (Chris's brother, William's son)

About the Authors:

The late William B. Gallagher spoke fluent Spanish, German, and Russian and could converse in French, Italian, and Portuguese. While in Viet Nam he picked up medical Vietnamese. He translated medical articles in many languages, including Romanian (using his knowledge of Italian) and Ukrainian (using his knowledge of Russian).

I (Chris) am fluent in Spanish, Italian, Portuguese, German, and French, can converse in Japanese, Mandarin, Swedish, Dutch, Russian, and Polish and have a limited (but pretty good) knowledge of Hebrew, Arabic, Serbo-Croatian, and Greek. Once, on a whim, I studied enough Icelandic to send my brother, Kim, a letter in this obscure language, just to freak him out. I have a lot of fun with languages.

Both my Dad and I concluded long ago that studying languages is a blast, opens doors, and does all sorts of cool stuff. Over our lifetimes, we've come up with tips, tricks, and methods to learn languages, lots of languages. We've also kept our ears and eyes open for great stories revolving around knowledge of a foreign language, and a lot of these stories involve *us* as the lingual protagonists!

Both of us have been asked this question, "How did you *learn* all those languages?"

Hence, the *existence* of this book.

We'll *tell* you how we learned all those languages, step

by step. To keep the book from getting too theoretical, we'll demonstrate by showing you how to learn Spanish, an awfully handy second language for anyone. The first part of the book will go through everything you need to become a...uh...cunning linguist yourself.

This first part will tell you the *how* part of speaking a foreign language.

The second part of the book will show you the *why* of speaking a foreign language.

How will we show you *why*? Why, by stories, that's how.

"No one likes a lecture but everybody likes a story", so, stories it is. Stories of how cool things happen when you speak a foreign language.

Hence, the *title* of this book.

These stories will emphasize *why* it's worth the effort to learn a language.

What kind of stuff happens when you have a few languages under your belt? Well, if you know...

- Russian. You run into a group of Russian sailors, recently rescued after a shipwreck, and you get to give the ship's doctor a home-made chocolate chip cookie. And shortly after that handoff, the Cold War comes to an end. Pretty heady stuff, this language business.

- Portuguese. You're working out at a track in Atlanta, and the entire Mozambique Olympic Team zips past you. Turns out you're the only American around who speaks their language (Portuguese!). So you have them over for dinner. How many people have Olympic Teams over for dinner?

- Spanish. When you complete an operation on a badly burned and scarred child in Ecuador, you come to appreciate a drinking straw like you've never appreciated anything before. You hear a "gracias" that you'll never forget. And on a different trip, when you're in Madrid, you save a woman from death by tetanus!

- German. You do a little detective work on the book *All Quiet on the Western Front* and figure out where the title came from. You might even live a *real life All Quiet on the Western Front* and use your knowledge of German to save your life and the life of your men, as my grandfather did.

- French. At a cafe in Paris, you hear history first-hand from someone who was there when it happened. History on the hoof.

- Italian. At a piazza in Rome, an Italian soldier tells you about his time in Beirut's civil war. And he says something you will never forget for the rest of your life.

How do I know that this kind of stuff happens? Because I've lived it. How do I know about that real life *All Quiet on the Western Front*? Because my Grandpa lived it, and Dad told me.

Are there worlds of language adventures waiting for you?

One way to find out. Hop on board and see for yourself *how* to learn a foreign language (we'll jump start you in Spanish). Then we'll show you how to jump from bilingual to multilingual, then you're off and running.

Somewhere, sometime soon, you will have your own linguistic "Aha!" moment, when your *own* language skills work their own magic. Then you won't need *our* stories, you'll have your own!

Who needs Harry Potter's magic wand? Your *speaking* will create magic.

Keep in mind, this *book* is not a magic wand. Language

3

learning is not a piece of cake, by any stretch. There is some hard work in store for you before the language magic happens. But this book is meant to **fire you up** about learning a language. If you can see the most useful tips in the HOW section, and you can see what cool stuff happens in the WHY section, you will become a linguist yourself.

We (well, me, Dad's gone now) want you to see what we saw a long time ago.

There is nothing cooler in the world than being a polyglot, a speaker of many tongues.

That's why we wrote this book, to make you *want* to speak a foreign language. To get you as maxed out about languages as we are. When you're stoked to do a task, no matter how difficult, you find a way.

Read this book, see what cool things happen when you speak a foreign language, and you'll be stoked too.

Along the way, we'll address some language myths and headaches:

- Why are Americans so bad at languages?
- Should you "learn Latin first"?
- How come everyone in Europe speaks three languages?
- "I took French for 5 years and can't ask for a glass of water."
- "I can't learn a language. I just don't have it in me."

How will we wrap all this up? Where else? At a cocktail party!

Think of the impression we'll make.

Vámonos, let's see how to learn Spanish.

HOW

Chapter 1

The Magnificent Seven

Let's get right to it and show you how the Gallaghers learn a language. Let's go with Spanish since that's one you're sure to use. Here are the "Magnificent Seven" recommendations that will get you speaking Spanish:

- No fear. The idea is to tear into the guts of Spanish, start practicing and working at it right away, today, before the sun sets. And never for a minute should you sweat the mistakes. Mistakes are the bricks of the Spanish house you're building. You'll need a lot of bricks, so start piling. The more *mistakes* you make, the faster you'll speak Spanish.

- 24/7 is ideal but admittedly unrealistic. Still, any time you can devote to language learning is to the good. You are now open to learning the language at all times in all places. No "one hour of language class a week" for you. If you overhear someone in the hall speaking Spanish, start speaking with them. If you see a sign in Spanish, read it.

- Everything at your disposal. From now on, at least part of every day, have your radio station playing in Spanish, one hour a day, have your television station in Spanish. While browsing the Internet, stop off at some Spanish speaking websites.

- If you have the dough, hire someone to practice with you. Go to a local community college and paste a sign up at the student union – "Talk Spanish with me, I'll pay." You'll get a call.

- Go to the bookstore or the library and get a bunch of different language learning packages. Books, books with accompanying CD's, books with computer programs. Get a bunch of them, use them all.

- Start making your own lessons by recording yourself. Buy a digital Dictaphone (they're 20 bucks or so at Radio Shack). Start recording yourself. Start listening to yourself. Congratulations, you are now not only a Spanish student, you are a Spanish instructor!

- Dual-language reading. This makes you take off like a rocket and amass vocabulary. The more words you know, the more you can talk. Get a dual-language short story book. After you go through that, then get a book you wanted to read anyway (*Harry Potter*, murder mystery, classic – as long as it's something with relatively simple vocabulary and a lot of dialogue). Buy the English version, and then get the Spanish version of it. (You can get Spanish books by ordering them on the Internet or else going to the Spanish sections of bookstores or libraries.) Read the two books side by side. One paragraph in English, then its corresponding paragraph in Spanish. Then one paragraph in Spanish, its corresponding paragraph in English. Back and forth.

Now let's go through each of the Magnificent Seven in more detail.

NO FEAR

Traditional teaching focuses on the RED PEN. The check mark next to the incorrect verb form, the points taken off for using the incorrect form of the plural, the bad grade for making too many wrong choices. This creates fear in the language student. Fear of the RED PEN, the points off, the bad grade.

The traditional solution? Play it safe. Never dare venture off the beaten path, the exact thing taught in class, the stuff you learned. Tiptoe into the language, staying on the straight and narrow, making sure you avoid the RED PEN at all costs. This will land you a good grade and lots of test papers free of red marks.

And that is fine and dandy if you are language student.

But you're *not* a language student, you are a *linguist*.

A linguist masters a language, a linguist doesn't care about the RED PEN. Linguists care about going from NOT knowing to KNOWING a language, and the sooner the better. And the way to do that is by getting rid of fear.

No fear.

Let's apply this to Spanish.

Say you know nothing about Spanish right now.

Go to Barnes and Noble, get a Spanish Phrase Book, open to page one, learn the phrase, "Buenos días." (Good morning).

On your way out of the store, you hear people speaking Spanish by the coffee section. As you walk by, smile and say, "Buenos días" to them.

Guess what, they'll say "Buenos días" back to you, and you've just had your first Spanish conversation.

But, but…but you don't know enough to have a conversation?

So what? The NO FEAR principle says you go for it even if you don't know much.

But…but…what if they keep talking back to you and you have no idea what they're saying. Won't that make you feel stupid?

So what? The NO FEAR principle says you venture out into the language, even if you're not assured of success. What the heck, just *trying* is success!

But…but…you haven't taken any classes or anything. You

don't have any formal training, so even speaking to these people is…I don't know, not right.

Who says? You're teaching yourself, you don't need classes, don't need formal anything. You're a linguist and you're going for it. Period. If you flounder and mispronounce and mix everything up, so what? Nobody died. No house burnt to the ground. You just made some grammar and vocabulary mistakes. So what? From these mistakes, you build up, you get better, you work your way towards mastery.

With NO FEAR as your motto, you plow ahead, always with your eyes on the prize.

Speaking the lingo.

A linguist has NO FEAR.

24/7

A language student takes a few hours of language class a week, at most. A linguist is on tap all the time for learning the language. Class is *always* in session. The learning *never* stops.

Let's use this with Spanish.

You're walking down the street, looking at cars.

How do you say street? (La calle)

How do you say cars? (Los coches)

You go into Starbucks and order a cappuccino. How would you say that in Spanish? (Un cappuccino, por favor.) Oh, guess what, you see that the person behind the counter is named Juan, take a chance.

"Un cappuccino, por favor."

You're in luck, he responds, "¡Como no!" You hadn't heard that before, it sounds like "Why no?" but that doesn't really make sense.

"Juan, what does that mean, '¡Como no!'?" you ask.

"Oh, that's kind of like 'Sure', or 'Why not, happy to'." Juan says.

"Great, thanks. ¡Como no!" (Always repeat what they say, it helps the phrase stick in your head.)

9

The next time you go in the Starbucks, you take it a little farther. You can say "Un cappuccino por favor" and that will land you a cup of steamy, frothy java, but you want to ask in a more complicated way. You want to stretch your wings.

"Dame un cappuccino." (Give me a cappuccino.)

"Hágame el favor de darme un cappuccino." (Do me the favor of giving me a cappuccino.)

"Quisiera un cappuccino." (I should like a cappuccino.)

So, each trip to Starbucks is a little exercise in "How can I express myself a little more than the last time?"

At home, the lessons go on.

You sit down to breakfast (look that up, it's "desayuno"), you drink your OJ (jugo de naranja), eat your toast (pan tostado) and eggs (heuvos). On Monday it was hard to name all these things, but you name them each time you eat them. By Thursday, desayuno, jugo de naranja, pan tostado, and huevos are all part of your active vocabulary, since you say (and eat!) them every day.

24/7 means "class is in session" when you go to Starbucks, when you eat your breakfast, when you're at work, when you're at play. 24/7 means you get something down, then you dig deeper. You know how to say something one way on Monday, you practice it on Tuesday and learn a more complicated way to say it on Wednesday.

24/7.

A linguist is relentless.

A linguist is always on.

EVERYTHING AT YOUR DISPOSAL

Put the Internet at your disposal.

The Internet has Spanish websites, radio, pod casts, and you name it. You are going to rope in everything Spanish off the Internet. News, weather, sports, everything.

Here's a little exercise.

Find out (in English) what the weather's going to be. Now, close out the English language website on your computer.

Hop over to the Spanish websites and find a weather report.

Guess what, the *languages* may vary but the reality of the *weather* is going to be the same. (Weather forecasters are inaccurate in all languages, but that's another issue.)

If the English language weather report says, "Rain, today." Then when you go over to Weather.com in Spanish, it'll say "Hoy, llueve." (Today, it rains.)

Do this same exercise regarding the news. If the English language news has pictures of the terrible bridge tragedy in Minneapolis, then the Spanish news will likely show a picture of the bridge with a headline, "Desastre en Minnesota" (Disaster in Minnesota.)

Guess what, the *languages* may vary but the reality of the *news* is going to be the same.

You may not speak much Spanish yet, but you are already using the language in a *context*. Spanish is a reality, so you look outside and see it's raining and that corresponds to the Spanish phrase you saw on the weather report (llueve – it's raining). The disaster in Minnesota is now "Un desastre en Minnesota" and it doesn't take a genius to see that "disaster" corresponds to "desastre" and you're already thinking in Spanish.

You put the Internet at your disposal and your vocabulary now includes "llueve" and "desastre" and you're going to remember them both. Your wet clothes will remind you what "llueve" means. That sad feeling when you think of the poor people on that bridge will remind you what "desastre" is.

Put the TV at your disposal.

Your TV has Spanish speaking channels. Turn them on and keep them on. Make your TV part of your "learn Spanish always and everywhere" world. If you can stomach the telenovelas (soap operas), then all the more power to you. (Even I, a dyed-in-the-wool linguist, can't stand watching that treacly pap no matter how much it improves my language skills.) The best way to jump start is watching the news. There's always a picture of the story, so you at least you have an idea of what's going on.

There's a picture of a flood in Bangladesh, houses underwater, people trying to escape a typhoon. The announcer is tearing along in Spanish but the word "inondación" keeps coming up. Hey, they even write it in big letters behind the announcer's head.

INONDACIÓN EN BANGLADESH.

Well, they're showing you a flood. They wrote a word up there that most likely means flood. "Inondación" seems pretty close to our "inundation", which is a fancy way of saying "flood." So guess what? Your vocabulary has just jumped by one more word. But it's not like you looked the word up in the dictionary and are trying to memorize it out of thin air. That word is attached to the vivid images of the rampaging floodwaters and the Bangladeshi people trying to escape the typhoon.

You put the TV at your disposal and now, and forever more, you know what "inondación" means.

Put the signs you see every day at your disposal.

Voting brochure at the election polls? What do you know, it's written in Spanish. Look it over. While you're at it, look over the signs all around.

"Vota aquí." (Vote here.) The English and the Spanish are right next to each other. It's a pretty safe guess that "vota" means "vote", so that leaves "aquí" to mean "here."

Two more words in your hip pocket. And two more words linked to an actual place (the voting booth) and an actual activity (casting your ballot). Those words, "Vota aquí" are going to stick.

In your office building, there's a sign near where they're

mopping, "Peligro, piso mojado." (Caution, wet floor.) OK, there are three more words to add to your vocabulary. If you want to make sure you never forget them, go ahead and step on the fresh wax, slip, and break a few bones. The linguist never spares him/herself! Anything to brand that lesson into the brain cells!

Put your car radio at your disposal. Spanish radio station? Listen to it. Even if you don't know what they're saying, you can still "tune your ear" to the sound of Spanish.

This is admittedly pretty tough, since you don't have INONDACIÓN EN BANGLADESH written behind the announcer to look at. But you still have that "link to reality" when they talk about the weather.

On the radio, they say, "Y ahora, el tiempo." With any luck, you pick up that this means, "And now, the weather."

Whatever they say next will translate into what you see hitting your windshield.

"Va a nevar hoy." (It's going to snow today.) That becomes an active vocabulary item as snowflakes swirl across your windshield.

"Va a llover hoy." (It's going to rain today.) That becomes an active vocabulary item as raindrops pelt your windshield.

"Un tsunami llega." (A tsunami is coming.) Let's hope this stays out of your active vocabulary and off your windshield.

Put your friends, neighbors, and co-workers at your disposal. (That sounds a little cold.) Let's put it this way, get your friends, neighbors, and co-workers on your "Learn Spanish" team.

Neighbors from Venezuela? Bring them a cake! Talk Spanish to them.

Someone at the office is from Mexico? Get the next round of coffee and donuts and start practicing with them.

A pal of yours did some Peace Corps work in El Salvador? Maybe his Spanish has gotten a little rusty but he wants to brush up on it. So brush up on it together.

Spanish speakers are *everywhere*. Take advantage of this! Each one of them can pitch into your studies, even a phrase or two each morning at the coffee shop or newspaper stand. Bare your soul to them.

-"Hey, I'm trying to learn a little Spanish, OK if I practice with you?"

-"It's pretty nice out today; let me see, you say, 'Hace buen tiempo' for that, right?"

-"'Me gusta tu camisa', I'm trying to say, 'I like your shirt', was that it?"

You will find yourself pleasantly surprised. Spanish speakers are tickled that you're making the effort and will be happy to pitch in to your education. There *may* be some exceptions to this, but my Dad never found one during his 82 year lifespan, and I've yet to see one during my 49 years. So that's 131 years total, and we are yet to see a Spanish speaker who doesn't want to help you learn!

(If you push on and go the multi-lingual route, we've got more good news. People in *every* language are tickled that you're trying and are also eager to help you learn.)

The linguist views *everything* and *everyone* as a means to mastery. The TV, the Internet, the iPod, the radio, the signs around you, the brochures, the neighbors, everything and everybody. Everything at your disposal.

The linguist is like the mountain climber, using every nook, cranny, and outcropping to help the ascent.

Everything at your disposal to get where you're going.

IF YOU HAVE THE DOUGH, HIRE
SOMEONE TO PRACTICE WITH YOU

How much money did you spend on our house? Your car? Your college education? Your stint in rehab?

Probably a lot. So why not fork out a little for your personal Spanish tutor?

College students are always looking for money. At one point I was having a terrible time learning the tones in Mandarin Chinese. I went to a local college campus, posted a sign on the Student Union, "Need someone to practice Chinese with, will pay for your time."

That night my phone rang. By the next week, I knew how to say the tones.

So go to your local community college, post a sign, "I need someone to practice Spanish with, will pay for your time."

Bingo, instant tutor.

You meet the first time, pull out a Spanish language newspaper, and point to the headline story, and say, "Could you please just read this aloud for me, I want to see how to pronounce Spanish."

Your personal tutor opens up and starts reading, "Hoy en la guerra en Iraq, George Bush vino a visitar." (Today in the Iraq war, George Bush came to visit.)

Now you take the paper and repeat the sentence, trying your best to imitate your personal tutor. "Hoy en la guerra in Iraq, George Bush vino a visitar."

Keep this up for a while until you're comfortable with your pronunciation.

Now, since this person is your personal tutor, take the lesson in any direction you want.

"Do me a favor, everything I say, say to me in Spanish."
"Hagame un favor, todo lo que digo, digame en español."

What do you know? Instant translation of the very stuff you want to know. Take it a step further; do "the opening conversation that you usually have with people." Go over the following stuff with your private tutor. Go over it again and again, and you'll be off to a good start.

Here's "the opening conversation you almost always have" in English:

Hello.
Hello.
How are you?
Fine.
You speak Spanish?
A little.
Really, where did you learn?
I taught myself.
That's amazing!

Here it is in Spanish. Write it out so you'll remember it and have your private tutor say it and practice it with you over and over.

Hola.
Hola.
¿Como está?
Bien.
¿Habla español?
Si.
De veras, ¿Donde aprendió?
Lo aprendí a mi mismo.
¡Que bueno!

The sentence in bold is the key to the kingdom. When the Spanish speaker finds out you learned by yourself, that will *knock their socks off*, and they will proceed to talk *more* with you.

Anyone who teaches him/herself a language must be damned interesting to talk to! That always comes through, always. It always raises an eyebrow, always raises the other person's interest, and always leads to more conversation.

(Same in every other language too, as I hope you'll find out.)

Even if you know *nothing else* in Spanish, learn this sentence

Lo aprendí a mi mismo.

That will *blow the doors off the conversation*, will convince whoever is talking to you that you are some kind of linguistic genius, and the conversation will go from there. Usually, the person talking to you will rope someone else in and pretty soon you'll have a battalion of Spanish speakers chattering away with you.

Doesn't matter that you don't understand anything they say! They will find a way to make themselves understood, or they will break into English every now and then. The main thing is you got them talking and you got them talking to *you*. That will start you on the road to speaking Spanish.

Let's take it a little further. What else do you need to know to burrow your way further into the language?

Hola — Hello
Hola. ¿Como está? — Hello. How are you?
Muy bien. ¿Habla español? — Very good. You speak Spanish?
Si, un poco, lo aprendí a mi mismo. — Yes, a little, I taught myself.

Now they descend on you, gather around, and start firing away and you are lost. Here's what you need to say to go a little further.

Perdón, no entiendo. — Excuse me, I don't understand.
Solo hablo un poquito. — I only speak a little.

This will unleash a torrent of protests, as all and sundry pour compliments on your fluency, regardless of how utterly lost you are.

¿Puede repitir? Un poco mas despacio, — Could you repeat? A little slower, please?

Remember, this is all stuff you go over with your personal tutor during your first session.

17

Be sure and write this down. Record it with a little Dictaphone. Practice each of these sentences yourself, then have the tutor say them as well, so you can see how it's supposed to sound.

Go back and forth, back and forth.

Learn these first lines the way an actor learns his lines in a play.

If you have to go over them 10 times, then go over them 10 times. If you have to "cheat and look at a piece of paper", then by all means cheat and look at a piece of paper.

THIS IS THE WAY THE FIRST CONVERSATION USUALLY GOES, SO LEARN IT BY HEART AND PRACTICE IT OVER AND OVER.

Back to reality now, you're still with your tutor. Your tutor is still on the clock, so let's go over the next few phrases that will help you out the most.

¿Que quiere decir eso? — What does that mean?

Literally, this means, "What does this want to say?", but it's how you say, "What does this mean?" Extremely useful phrase! Anytime anybody says anything you don't understand, you can jam on the linguistic brakes and "back up" by saying "¿Que quiere decir eso?"

What's the flip side of that expression? When you want to say something in Spanish but you just do not have the vocabulary, point to something and say:

¿Como se dice eso? — How do you say that?
(You point to a window.)
Como se dice eso? — How do you say that?
Ventana. — Window.
Ventana. — Window.

Note the **Ventana** in bold letters. That is YOU repeating what the Spanish speaker said. Don't just let *them* say it, *you* say it too. That allows you to mimic the sound they make (they pronounce perfectly, after all, it's *their* language), allows them to correct you if you make a mistake and this also cements the word in your head. You look at the window, you hear them say ventana, you yourself say ventana – that word should stick!

Alas, the fun should go on forever, but at some point you'll have to take your leave. Pull these out of your hip pocket.

Mucho gusto. — Nice meeting you.
Hasta luego. — See you later.

Keep your eyes peeled for Spanish speakers in your world. Maybe there are a few Spanish speakers who always wait for the same train you do. Strike up a conversation with them! In your office, your school, your neighborhood, somewhere *near* and somewhere you *go a lot*, there are probably people who speak Spanish. Make friends with them and use this "beginning conversation" that you just learned with your personal tutor.

Remember the crucial sentence that ALWAYS generates a buzz:

Lo aprendí a mi mismo.

You will get a lot of mileage out of that little sentence!

Now, work with your tutor on the following phrases:

Buenos días. — Good morning.
Buenas tardes. — Good afternoon.
Buenas noches. — Good evening.

With those, you'll be able to launch more encounters.

¿Come está? — How are you?
Muy bien, gracias — Very well, thanks.
Hace buen tiempo hoy — Nice weather we're having.

Standard icebreakers. Even if the weather's terrible, say, "Hace buen tiempo hoy." That'll get a laugh! The irony of it! (Now you'll *really* seem fluent, you can even *joke* in Spanish.)

Me llamo (put in your name here). — My name is (X)
¿Como se llama? — What is your name?

Now pause and take a big breath. Before you plunge further and start shorting out your brain, go back and review these simple sentences. These few sentences are often all you need to know for most conversations. (The train arrives, work starts, class begins, and people have to break off the conversation.) So guess what? If you just know these few phrases, and that's all you end up saying, guess what? You're fluent!

What? Fluent with just a half dozen phrases?

Yes! With the help of your tutor, and learning a few key phrases, you were able to make yourself understood and you were able to understand what was said. If that isn't fluent, then what is? THIS IS A KEY ELEMENT TO STARTING OFF IN SPANISH, OR ANY LANGUAGE. You don't need a million word vocabulary for most of your "sociable" conversations. With a relatively modest "supply" of words, you can "meet and greet" quite well.

You wanted to speak Spanish, and after one little lesson with your personal tutor, guess what you're doing? You are speaking Spanish! You are doing it! Who cares you say four sentences then run out of steam. At least you spoke four sentences!

This will fire you up to work further with your tutor. This initial success will give you the mental jet fuel you need to go further and study more. Success builds success. It's the fire in your heart that will get you speaking Spanish. It's that feeling of "Wow, I actually did this, I actually had a conversation" that will get you revved to learn more.

Here's the "more" you'll need to go a little further. Maybe work on this with your second session with your personal tutor.

Soy de (your hometown). — I'm from (hometown).
¿De donde es? — Where are you from?

Everyone wants to know where everyone is from. It's the natural progression of most initial conversations. If you can "see ahead" to what most people say to each other most of the time, you can "map out" just about any conversation.

So map it out and practice it with your friendly neighborhood tutor. (Even if you've used up a few hours by now, it's still way less than you paid for your car!)

I'll give you my initial conversation that plays out again and again, all in Spanish. (Obviously, you'd fill in your own personal information instead of mine.) I'll talk in italics, the Spanish person I just met will be in regular font. You would go over this with your tutor playing first one role, then the other, so you'd get both sides of the conversation down.

Buenos días. — Good morning.
Buenos días. — Good morning
¿Como está? — How are you?
Bien, ¿y Usted? — Fine, you?
Muy bien, gracias. — Very good, thanks.

By this point in the conversation, any Spanish speaker has pegged me for a gringo because of my accent. So the conversation, naturally, turns to how this gringo comes to speak the lingo.

¿Donde aprendió español? — Where did you learn Spanish?
Lo aprendí a mi mismo. — I taught myself.

This, as noted earlier, always raises an eyebrow, as few people teach themselves languages! So, to come across as self-deprecating and "just plain folks", it's good at this point to take yourself down a peg.

Lo aprendí en un carcel en Tijuana. — I learned it in a Tijuana jail.

That always brings down the house.

¿Que haces? — What do you do? (The idea is, what is your profession?)
Soy medico. — I'm a doctor.

Here's where you map out your own personal comeback. Whatever you are, butcher, baker, candlestick maker, rich man, poor man, beggar man, thief, look up how to say it in a dictionary.

Soy professor de inglés. — I'm an English professor.
Soy estudiante. — I'm a student.
Soy espión. — I'm a spy.

Have at your disposal and in your active vocabulary all the information that people are likely to want to know about you. Let's go back to my version of things so you can see it in action. We'll pick it up at

Soy medico. — I'm a doctor.
¿Que tipo? — What kind?
Un medico muy guapo. — A very handsome doctor.

Go ahead, build in your own jokes! The one about the "jail in Tijuana" gets'em every time, as does the "handsome doctor" one. Doesn't matter that I've used them a million times. This *particular* person has never heard it before. The corny little jokes help propel the conversation along, break the ice a little. We were perfect strangers a few sentences ago, but now we've shared a few laughs, so that will move the conversation a little deeper.

To repeat and re-emphasize the importance of your tutor: you map this whole thing out and *practice it to distraction* with your tutor.

Where do we go after the handsome doctor?

¿De donde es? — Where are you from?
Soy de Wisconsin, cerca de Chicago. — *I'm from Wisconsin, near Chicago.*
¿De donde es? — Where are you from?

In Spanish, like in any language, getting asked about yourself implies, "Do you want to know about me too?" So make sure you have your own "ask back" questions ready to go.

¿Es casado? — Are you married.
Sí, ¿ y Usted? — *Yes, and you?*
¿Tiene hijos? — Do you have kids?
Sí, una hija. ¿Y Usted? — *Yes, a daughter, and you?*

A lot of becoming a linguist is just employing common courtesy and basic conversational skills. Since this is what you would say to someone in *English* if you first met them, this is what you should practice and memorize in Spanish. You're *sure* to use it.

Back to your interaction with your tutor:
How many lessons will it take to nail down this initial conversation? Depends. Maybe 4 hours or so. Say you pay your tutor $25/hr (all cash, Uncle Sam doesn't need to know about this). Toss in a tip and picking up the tab at Starbucks, you've laid out $100 and change to master a decent starting Spanish conversation.

$100 and change!

You drop that at a medium dinner with friends, and that's before drinks. Is it worth one medium dinner to sink your fangs into a language and get off to a good start?

The linguist says yes. Best 100 dollar investment you've ever made.

Keep seeing that tutor a few times a week, a few hours every now and then, and talk about anything – family, events of

23

the day, sports, music. Just as you mapped out and practiced a generic "ice breaker" conversation, you can map out any other conversation you might need:

-Business deal.
-Chess.
-Golf.
-Art history.

That's the beauty of your *own* tutor. The lesson learned will always be on a subject *you* want to learn.

Minor investment in money, big payoff in your Spanish!

GO TO THE BOOKSTORE OR LIBRARY AND GET A BUNCH OF LANGUAGE LEARNING MATERIAL

Go back to the earlier questions about money. How much money did you spend on your house? Your car? Your college education? Your stint in rehab?

About a bazillion dollars, right?

Now go wild, go hog wild in the bookstore and get a bunch of different language books, CD's, DVD's. Get a *Teach Yourself Spanish* book, a phrase book a book on verbs. What's the most you'll drop, even if you get *everything* on the shelf? Maybe a few hundred bucks?

Not an insignificant amount, I'll admit, but not a lot compared to what you're paying in property tax this month, or your kid's college tuition, is it?

Low on dough? Make the same "shopping trip" at your local public library. The price is *always* right at the library.

What's the idea of getting a *bunch* of different learning packages? Isn't one better than the others, shouldn't one suffice?

Short answer, "No."

Each language course touts itself as the best. That makes sense; each language course wants you to buy *their* course and not someone else's.

I have a different take on that.

Get any of them, they're all good. They all teach in their own way and all help you learn in a slightly different way.

Language courses are like exercise equipment: as long as you USE it and WORK it; they're *all* good for you.

- Got an exercise bike? If you ride it, you'll get fit. Your "biking muscles" will get fit.
- Bow-flex? Work at it, and you'll end up chiseled and lean like the people on the commercials.
- Ab-o-sizer? Work it; your abs will get fit.
- Thigh Master? Work at it, you'll be able to crush walnuts with your thighs.
- Jump rope? Work it; your cardio fitness will soar.

What if you get and work all of them?
You'll be killer. You'll be the bomb.

Same goes for the language courses.

- *Spanish in Three Months*. It has CD's included to help you master pronunciation. Good lessons, progressively difficult conversations. Clear explanations. Work it, you'll learn Spanish.
- *Teach Yourself Spanish*. Also available with CD's. Same deal. Starts out simple, gets progressively more challenging. Great stuff. Work it, you'll learn Spanish.
- *Rosetta Stone*. Great visuals on your computer. You pick the right answer out of four pictures and pretty soon you are *thinking* in Spanish. Work it, you'll learn Spanish.
- *Pimsleur*. Just listen and repeat. They go over things so many times you are able to say complicated

sentences before you know it. Work it (especially in your car or while exercising) and you'll learn Spanish.

- *201 Spanish Verbs* and, if you get ambitious, its big brother, *501 Spanish Verbs*. When you get to the point that you want to take on additional verb forms and tenses, this lays it all out for you. Plus, there are sample sentences at the bottom of the page that help show the "verbs in action." Work it, you'll learn Spanish.

- *Spanish Phrase Book*. There are tons of these. Great for when you're starting out. There'll be a section on restaurants, you can bring it into the Mexican restaurant, and just jump to the phrase you want to say. Work it, you'll learn Spanish.

What if you get and work all of them?
You'll be killer. You'll be the bomb.

Any *one* course gets to be a bit of a drag after a while. And you *never* want your interest to flag. So by having a bunch of learning material, you can go from course to course, each one augmenting and reviewing what you learned in the other courses.

Picture yourself like a skier, slaloming through the various courses.

- Start out with a phrase book. They spell out how to say everything. That will give you:
  Yes (sí), no (no), buenos días (good morning), and ¿Como está Usted? (How are you?)
  Once you've gotten a few phrases down and tried them out in the real world (start talking right away!), now you're ready to "hone your ear" a little more.

- Listen to *Pimsleur* in the car on your way to work.

- Go over a *Rosetta Stone* course on your home computer. Both *Rosetta Stone* and *Pimsleur* will start you "thinking in the language" as well as helping your pronunciation. Imitate what you hear. (That's how babies learn to talk, after all.)

- Now you have a few phrases down and a little pronunciation skill. Crack open a *Teach Yourself Spanish* book or a *Spanish in Three Months* course. You'll start getting the building blocks of the grammar so you can make up your own phrases. You'll see in print the stuff you heard on *Pimsleur* and you'll have an "Aha!" moment or two.

- Listen to the *Pimsleur* course again. The stuff will really stick the second time around.

- Review *Rosetta Stone*.

- Keep going through the *Teach Yourself Spanish* book.

- Slalom, slalom, slalom.

- Now you can look at that *201 Spanish Verbs* book. Pluck out the verbs you've used a lot (speak – hablar, go – ir, eat – comer, read – leer). Now's the time to "stretch your wings" a little and get down more complicated verb tenses.

- Back to the phrase book. Hey, the grammar and tenses in these set expressions now make sense! It's no longer just rote memorization.

- *Pimsleur* and *Rosetta* have advanced courses. Go for it!

- Slalom, slalom.

If you keep jumping around like this, going from method to method, you're less likely to burn out and get stalled. Every time something gets to be a drag jump to an alternative method.

They're *all* teaching you Spanish, so they're *all* to the good.

No athlete does just one exercise, they all cross train. No gym has just one piece of equipment. You, the Spanish-speaking athlete, should follow suit. Get a whole batch of learning tools and cross train your way to fluency.

START MAKING YOUR OWN LESSONS BY RECORDING YOURSELF

Get your own Dictaphone. (They're cheap as dirt and hold a hundred hours or so of recording.)

Make your OWN language lesson, using the phrases you use every day. The first time you meet with your tutor, record yourself saying that crucial "first conversation that everybody has." Record the tutor as well, so you can check your pronunciation.

Then, at home, think up more conversations you might have, and record them too. Once you've recorded them, listen to them. That way, you've:

-thought of the conversation

-spoken it

-listened to it

Three separate mental exercises. That's one lesson you'll remember!

Let's make up another Starbucks lesson. (I love that place, as several inches around my waistline will attest to.)

You get up, go to Starbucks, and ask for a cappuccino. Now how would I say that in Spanish? (Say you were in a Starbucks in Mexico City.)

"Por favor, un cappuccino. Gracias." Please, a cappuccino. Thanks.

OK, simple as simple can be, but it gets the message across. Now record that on your own Dictaphone. Later on, you can listen to it (building up your "receiving" skill).

What else might you say in Starbucks?

"Where's the bathroom?" *"¿Donde estan los servicios?"*
OK, record it. Listen to it.

"¿Donde estan los servicios?" "Where's the bathroom?"

Receiving, sending. And all from your own efforts. Early on, you may want to record *both sides of the conversation*, so you can *understand* Spanish when *spoken to*, and so you can *create* Spanish when the need arises.

OK, we got our cappuccino, now let's sit down at the table and think for a little while about this whole receiving – sending idea. This is a crucial item to understand.

Receiving lesson. Can I *understand* Spanish when I *hear* it?
"Donde estan los servicios?" That means, "Where is the bathroom?"

Sending lesson. Can I *create* Spanish when I *need* it?
I want to say, "Where's the bathroom? *"¿Donde estan los servicios?"*

Record it both ways. Listen to it both ways. Listen to the phrase where the Spanish is spoken first (receiving) and where English is spoken first (sending). Using the Dictaphone is great for making sure you get Spanish in both receiving and sending mode. Let's develop this a little more.

As time passes, you will hit certain walls:
-How do I say this in a more complicated way?
-How would I say this in the past tense?
-How would I say this if there were more than one of us here?
Use your Dictaphone to record yourself as you overcome these walls. Work with your tutor or your language learning books to solve the problems, then record it all. Now, in your mind's eye, you're getting up from the table and going back to

the counter, ready for another cup of cappuccino.

How would I ask in a more complicated way?

Instead of saying, "Por favor, un cappuccino. Gracias", you're adding a little more lingo and saying, "Buenos días, ¿Como está? Hoy quisiera un cappuccino por favor." (Good morning, how are you? Today I should like a cappuccino please.)

Let's record it both ways, receiving and sending.

Receiving lesson. Can I *understand* this phrase when I *hear* it?

"Buenos días, ¿Como está? Hoy quisiera un cappuccino por favor."

This means, "Good morning. How are you? Today I should like a cappuccino please."

Sending lesson. Can I *create* this phrase when I *need* it?

"Good morning. How are you? Today I'd like a cappuccino please."

To convey this, I'd say, "Buenos días, ¿Como está? Hoy quisiera un cappuccino por favor."

This might come across as a little clumsy, actually saying "Sending lesson, can I create this phrase when I need it?" Then you go ahead and say the entire sentence in English and then in Spanish. But guess what, it works! This method gets your mind working both ways, understanding Spanish when it's coming in, and creating Spanish when it's time to send it *out*.

And all this on your little Dictaphone!

Let's overcome the second little wall.

How would I say this in the past tense? OK, imagine yourself describing what happened *yesterday* at Starbucks when you were in line. Put it in the "receive" and "send" mode, and you'll come up with this:

Receiving lesson. Can I *understand* this when I *hear* it?

"Ayer, dije, 'Buenos días, ¿Como está? Quisiera un cappuccino por favor."

Which means, "Yesterday, I said, 'Good morning. How are you? I should like a cappuccino please.'"

Sending lesson. Can I *create* this when I *need* it?

"Yesterday, I said, 'Good morning. How are you? I should like a cappuccino please."

Which, in Spanish, is, "Ayer, dije, 'Buenos días, ¿Como está? Quisiera un cappuccino por favor."

Not a huge difference. All you did was add, "Ayer, dije" (Yesterday, I said). But that's how you build up your skill. Add a little here and there. Little additions that beef your Spanish up.

Let's overcome that last little wall.

How would I say this if there were more than one of us? OK, imagine two of you in line at Starbuck's and both of you want cappuccino. Here goes the next little recording in your Dictaphone:

Receiving lesson. Can I *understand* this when I *hear* it?

"Buenos días. ¿Como está? Quisieramos dos cappuccinos por favor."

Which means, "Good morning.' How are you? We should like two cappuccinos please."

Sending lesson. Can I *create* this when I *need* it?

"Good morning. How are you? We should like two cappuccinos please."

Which, in Spanish, is "Buenos días. ¿Como está? Quisieramos dos cappuccinos por favor."

Record it. Listen to it. Listen to it again. Did you notice one "stealth" benefit of making all these little changes? With each version, you made one little change, but you also repeated the phrases that didn't change. You repeated the "background" parts.

"Buenos días."
"¿Como está?"
"Por favor."

The "background" words in your little exercise were reviewed again and again. You weren't even *thinking* about them, (they weren't a "wall" to be overcome). But there they were. Each time. And each time you *received* them (heard them in Spanish and figured out what they meant in English). And each time you *sent* them (thought of them in English and created the Spanish).

Only, truth to tell, you didn't even have to *think* about it by the end, did you? They just, sort of, fell into place.

You are becoming a linguist.

DUAL-LANGUAGE READING

This gets you the farthest the fastest.

1. **Get a dual-language book. Since we're focusing on Spanish, get a book called *Cuentos Españoles*. On the left side, the story is in Spanish. On the right side, the story is in English. You read a paragraph in Spanish, then cross over and read the paragraph in English. Now, read the next paragraph in English, cross over, and read the paragraph in Spanish. At first, especially early in your learning, not much will make sense. But as you work your way through the stories, you'll see "the common words occurring commonly." And guess what? The common words are the ones you'll need the most, since you *use* them the most. The common words take on the same "automatic entry into your brain" as the "background phrases" did in your Dictaphone exercises.**

2. **Get a Spanish version of a simple story. (On the Internet, you can order Spanish books, plus, bookstores and libraries all have Spanish language sections.) For example, get the children's-but-adults-enjoy-it-too book *The Little Prince*. In Spanish, *El Principito*. Now, lay the books side-by-side and read them just like you would the dual-language book.**

El principito dijo… — The Little Prince said…
El gigante dijo… — The Giant said…

As your eye goes down the page, you read first in Spanish, then you go over to the English version and read the translation. What keeps you reading is the story itself. You're not just pounding through a grammar text, you are reading an interesting story, and the language is coming along for the ride.

Once you've gotten down *El Principito*, move on to other books that you like. Stick with books with relatively easy vocabulary, preferably something with a lot of dialogue. Plus, you want to find a book that is easy to find in Spanish. Agatha Christie mysteries are a favorite of mine. Easy to find in English, easy to find in Spanish, plenty of dialogue, easy grammar (they're not dense tracts of philosophy or differential equations, after all), plus the story "carries you along." Whodunit, after all, is a pretty compelling question, and Agatha Christie knows how to keep you guessing.

Harry Potter in English and Spanish? Sure, it's a great story. It's kind of fun, too, to see how they translate made-up words like Quidditch and the various bizarre spells that Harry casts.

Da Vinci Code in English and Spanish? Good story, keeps you guessing, keeps you on the edge of your seat, lot of dialogue. One special treat in translations of *Da Vinci Code* involves the various word puzzles in the story. How do you translate an anagram? It's a kick to see how they do it.

And always the common words appear again and again.

So, as you read, you will get exposed MOST to the very words you'll *hear* and *speak* the most.

For example, in the Agatha Christie books, you'll see the word dijo a lot. It means "he said" or "she said."

Because in Agatha Christie books, there's a ton of dialogue, with a lot of this business:

"I took the knife down," he said. (In the Spanish version, it'll say "dijo" here.)
"Then you must have killed the vicar," she said. (Dijo.)
"No, he fell on the knife by accident," he said. (Dijo.)
"I shan't believe such poppycock", she said. (Dijo.)

You might not remember all the other stuff, but at the end of each sentence, you'll see "dijo", which means "he said" or "she said." That's a common word, used all the time, and in this short stretch of four sentences, you have seen it four times. Without even *thinking* about it, the word "dijo" has just entered your vocabulary because you've seen it so often. (Again, remember the "background phrases" in your Dictaphone exercise.)

If a murder occurs in a library, you'll see "biblioteca" appear a hundred times in the book. Guess what? That's *library*. And that's the beauty of the side by side approach. You fatten up your vocabulary, but you do it in a fun, painless way. There's no "write the word down, cover it up, memorize it", rather, you drift along in the book, seeing the words over and over, seeing the words in the context of a story, and the words slip into your memory banks.

And all the time you're reading a book - a good investment of your time in any language!

"The Magnificent Seven" are a great start for any language, and they'll be a great start for you as you learn Spanish.

- No Fear.
- 24/7
- Everything at your disposal.
- If you have the dough, hire a personal tutor.
- Get a bunch of learning material.
- Start recording yourself.
- Side by side reading.

What's the karma behind "The Magnificent Seven"?

Language learning is an extreme sport! Go at it with the same over-the-top enthusiasm you would give to mountain climbing or kayaking or triathlons. This is no mollycoddled, leaf-through-dusty-tomes effort, this activity kicks!

Next, you'll have to take on "The Grammar Monster."

Chapter 2

Slaying the Grammar Monster

Pretty soon you're going to run up against the **grammar monster**. You'll be a little spooked at first, because people have given grammar a bad name. Nothing of the sort! Here's a way to put grammar in perspective.

WHY YOU NEED GRAMMAR, THE POLLY THE PARROT PARADIGM

Polly the Parrot is too clever by half. On *Animal Planet*, they have talent shows where Polly (and her many cousins) display an amazing repertoire:

> *"Polly wants a cracker."*
> *"Go away!"*
> *"Somewhe-e-ere, over the rainbow."*
> *"Get down, get funky."*

Polly can even pick up cues and answer correctly:

"Polly, who's your boyfriend?"
  "Elvis."
"What should you stay off of?"
"Stay off a my blue suede shoes."

But Polly, no matter how fascinating, is still a birdbrain (uh, literally) because Polly can only imitate, she can't create stuff on her own.

Polly doesn't know grammar.

So Polly can sing songs from *The Wizard of Oz* or from Elvis records. She can repeat profanity and pick up cues. She can delight, amaze, and keep your attention for many a minute.

But she doesn't know grammar.

If you steer around grammar, viewing it as some evil three-headed serpent, you will forever be stuck in "Polly-land." You'll be able to repeat, imitate, keep the language afloat for some minutes, but you'll run out of gas as soon as you wander off the script.

Grammar allows you to make up new stuff and allows you to recognize things you haven't heard before. Grammar is not some dusty thing "outside" the language, grammar IS the language.

Let's snap our fingers and let Polly master grammar. Where could Polly go with this new linguistic weapon?

"Polly want a cracker?"

"No, Polly (and I prefer you not address me in the third person), prefers a ruff of braised dandelion leaves with cilantro vinaigrette on the side. Make sure the lettuce is union-picked."

"Whoa, Polly, getting pretty fancy on us, aren't you?"

"Crackers are high carb, and, for that matter, not the good carbs. If Polly, that is, I, am ever going to reattain my girlish figure, I'm going with the South Beach Diet and that means ix-nay on the arbs-cay ."

It's a new life for Polly! Grammar has opened up all sorts of new vistas for Polly the Now-Loquacious Parrot! Let's see what Spanish grammar can do for you.

Here's the Spanish grammar you need to know. Like earlier chapters, we'll focus on what you *need* to know rather than doing some exhaustive treatment of *everything under the sun*. Some of this will incorporate "The Magnificent Seven." Now give Polly a cracker to keep her quiet while you tame the grammar monster.

Ten Tricks and Tips to Tame the Grammar Monster:

1. **First learn how to pronounce the letters, so you can read aloud and start training your ear.**
2. **Learn a few crucial greetings so you can "get off the ground."**

3. Seek a "nearby native speaker." (Someone at work or living nearby.)

4. Start using your language as soon as possible; don't "wait until you're good."

5. Just learn the "I" and "you" forms of verbs initially. They're the forms you will use the most.

6. Just learn the present and past of the verbs initially. Leave more complicated tenses for later.

7. "Slalom" through the different learning methods. Learn a few phrases from a phrase book without worrying about the grammar. Then go into a grammar book until you understand how the phrases were made. Then slalom into a simple book so your vocabulary fattens up a little. Keep moving from method to method, don't allow yourself to stall out.

8. All the time, keep that Spanish radio station on, keep that Spanish television station on (at least part of the day) to keep honing your ears.

9. Record yourself, listen to yourself, record yourself, and listen to yourself.

10. Cultivate friendships with Spanish speakers, go to Spanish festivals, and immerse yourself.

Let's put these into action in Spanish to see how it's done.

1. First learn how to pronounce the letters, so you can read aloud and start training your ear.

Lucky us, Spanish is pretty easy to pronounce. Each letter has just one sound, unlike English, which has a million exceptions and arcane rules. The only letters that are going to give you trouble are the "r" and the "rr."

(Interesting side note – the pronunciation of "r" is one of the most challenging problems in speaking all sorts of languages. Put another way, an American with a bad accent in a foreign language is most often identified by the poor pronunciation of the "r.")

The Spanish phrase "Para ti" (for you) is a good phrase to study. It should sound like "pahda tee." The "r" is like a lightly tapped "d." Believe it or not, it should sound exactly like a fast pronunciation of "pot o' tea." Not "pot OH tea", but a quick "pahda tea."

The other toughie is the "rr" which is rolled. People old enough to remember the "Rrrrruffles have rrrrrridges" potato chip commercial were treated to a perfect pronunciation of the "rr" sound. It sounds like a bunch of "d's" run together. Some people, adult learners especially, just plain can't do it. Cause for concern? Never! The linguist never sees a stumbling block as a blind alley. A stumbling block is just something you work around! If you pronounce the rest of Spanish pretty well and can't quite get the "r" or "rr" sound down too well, then you'll just be speaking Spanish with an accent.

I'm going to forego a painful rendition of all the rest of the letters, this is where you go to a native speaker or listen to one of those CD's.

2. Learn a few crucial greetings so you can "get off the ground."

What's the goal of the linguist? What's the goal of the budding Spanish speaker?

To talk to someone in Spanish! So, there's no getting around the social conventions and niceties that govern us. You'll have to say hello, you'll have to introduce yourself, and you'll have to ask how the other person's doing. You'll notice along the way in these chapters that "the common things get repeated." Is this a good thing? Yes! We repeat the common things in this book because in the real world, the *common things will occur commonly*, so you want to review them.

A surprising number of conversations will go this far and no further. If you're able to pull off these few phrases without a hitch, and the conversation stops there, you will come across as "fluent in Spanish" since you will have carried out the complete interchange in Spanish.

You'll make a great impression even if your entire vocabulary consists of these words and no others!

"Hola." (Hello).

The Spanish speaker responds, "Hola."

So far so good! You've had your first conversation. You handled the expressive part fine and managed the receptive part just as well. Pat yourself on the back!

"Me llamo Chris." (Pronounced 'may yamo Krees' – My name is Chris.)

The Spanish speaker responds, "Me llamo Don Quixote." (Pronounced 'may yamo don keehotay' – My name is Don Quixote).

Wow, the people you meet!

"¿Como está?" (Pronounced como estah – How are you?)

"Muy bien, gracias." (From now on we'll skip the pronunciation, since you'll be able to do it by yourself in no time.)

Done!

Yes, the conversation could go on. But, for now, let's just stick with this.

Greeting – "Hola." There are more complicated greetings, but, when you're starting, always stick with the easiest-to-remember, simplest version.

Introduction – "Me llamo Chris." (My name is Chris.)

Polite inquiry – "¿Como está?" (How are you?)

Believe it or not, you want to hang on this simplest of conversations for a little. Say it over and over, record it, and practice it. This and no more. Just that tiny little start of every conversation that you will always use and will always need.

Hola.
Me llamo Chris.
¿Como está?

Practice it like a basketball player practices lay-ups or the way a singer does scales. It's the first thing you'll always use, so have it down pat. *Add* to it; yes, but always be ready to go *back* to it.

You will notice a surprising thing when you first go "out there" ready to flash around your language skill. No matter how much you've worked and how much complicated stuff you know, when the moment of truth comes, you will find yourself "freezing up." Your 500 word vocabulary will instantly shrink to about 5 words, you won't be able to dredge up any grammar, your tongue will stick to the roof of your mouth, and you'll stand there like a gasping fish, moving the mouth, but no words coming out.

DON'T SWEAT IT, IT HAPPENS TO EVERYBODY. This is part of the linguist's journey – the "initial attempt goes South." The important thing is – you made the attempt. So you plow through it, and you do another attempt, and another and another. And eventually you don't freeze up; rather, you start to loosen up and get comfortable with the language.

But when that first freeze occurs, go back to that crucial, multiply-practiced set of basic phrases you always need to start things going.

Hola.
Me llamo Chris (obviously, put in your name!)
¿Como está?

3. Seek a "nearby native speaker." (Someone at work or living nearby.)

You do not need to live in Southern California or Brownsville,

Texas or Miami to find a native speaker of Spanish. Spanish speakers are everywhere in America.

Here's how I did it. You can use your work/home circumstances to do the same thing.

The people who do our lawn are from Mexico. How do I know? I heard them speaking Spanish and asked them, "¿De donde son?" (Where are you from?)

"Mexico."

Anytime they're doing the lawn and I'm around, I go out and talk to them.

Guy delivers the pizza, has a Spanish accent. He's from Cuba. Talked with him for a bit.

At the hospital, lot of people from South America and the Caribbean. Make a point of knowing where they're from and you've got yourself a Spanish tutor every time you turn around.

IF YOU KNOW SOMEONE AND THEY SPEAK SPANISH, SPEAK SPANISH TO THEM, DON'T GET LAZY AND FALL INTO ENGLISH JUST BECAUSE WE'RE HERE IN THE U.S. OF A.

You know them, you see them every day, there is absolutely no pressure to "say things right." You may even find yourself (as I did) telling them, "Quando hago un error, por favor, dígame." (When I make a mistake, please tell me.) A lot of times, they'll let mistakes slide and won't feel polite correcting you. So ask them to correct you!

We do the same thing. If a recent immigrant asked you, "Coffee want drink. Where go?" You would most likely point them to the cafeteria or the nearby Starbucks; you wouldn't correct their grammar mistakes. There were a lot of mistakes, but you still understood what they wanted.

When we tell a Spanish speaker, "Café querer beber. ¿ Donde ir?" we've sounded the same as the "Coffee want drink. Where go?" person. And most likely, the Spanish speaker would point to the cafeteria or Starbucks and wouldn't correct our grammar mistakes either.

Once you open your eyes, the possibilities for practicing Spanish are endless. (Later on, when we take on learning *multiple* languages, you may be surprised to find out that most of us live in a Tower of Babel, with language opportunities all around us.)

-The secretary at Human Resources is from Venezuela, talk to her when you pass near her desk.

-Your dentist was born in Chile and moved here when he was 8 so he has no accent, but he speaks fluent Spanish. Talk with him – before he puts all that dental equipment in your mouth.

Snoop around. A little detective work will reveal a host of Spanish speakers all around you. If you just ask "Where are you from, originally?" you may find a dozen Spanish speakers before the sun goes down tonight.

And once you've opened up a little door with that language effort, the payoff goes on in terms of friendships, all kinds of good stuff.

When you make the effort to "reach out and touch someone" in their native language, you have paid them a tremendous compliment:

-"I care enough about your culture and your background to start learning your language."

And you're reaching out to them in another way; you're asking for their help:

-"I'm trying to learn your language, can you help me a little?"

That's a great one-two punch for building bridges – complimenting a person's background and then asking them for their help and expertise. I have used this approach myself with hundreds of people and nearly a dozen languages. In Spanish, and, without exception, all the other languages, this is a great way to make connections with people. And it's a great way to improve your language. I've made a lot of Spanish-speaking friends this way and learned a lot of Spanish. And I'm still learning.

One way to make sure the conversation is always "spicy" is to know how to "push a few hot button topics." Try this with your new Spanish speaking friends.

Every country thinks they speak THE BEST Spanish. This is always a hot button topic. Asking about this will *always* get Spanish speakers talking. As a side benefit, it's kind of fun to buy into this whole debate. Stoking the flames of this debate is a blast. Here's what I've picked up so far. Of course, it's all deeply prejudiced, since everyone puts down the other countries and sings the praises of their own country.

From a Columbian: "Nuestro accento es el mas rafinado." (Our accent is the most cultured.) "¿Los Cubanos? Ay, comen los eses, nadie puedo entenderlos." (The Cubans? Oh, they eat their 's's'. Nobody can understand them.)

From a Puerto Rican (famous for talking very fast, and they do!): "Hablamos mas rapido porque tenemos muchas cosas a decir." (We talk fast because we have a lot to say.)

From a Chilean, putting down nearby Argentina (which has a reputation for conceit): "¿Sabes porque un argentino sonríe cuando sale en el sol? Porque cree que Dios saca su fotografia." (Do you know why an Argentinian smiles when he goes out on a sunny day? He thinks God is taking his photograph.)

It goes on and on.

So every Latin country puts down every other one. All in good fun, of course. (They *have* occasionally gone to war against each other, but these things happen.)

So take advantage of this ongoing "ribbing each other." When you make the acquaintance of a Mexican, ask them, "Se habla mejor en Mexico o en Guatemala?" (Do they speak better in Mexico or in Guatemala?) You've just guaranteed yourself 30 minutes of free conversation!

4. Start using your language as soon as possible; don't "wait until you're good."

It's tough to jump into a cold pool. You stick your toe in, maybe your whole foot, and you have a sudden bond with all those Titanic people who had to jump into the icy North Atlantic.

Maybe I'll just wait here a little bit.

So you stand there with your ankle in the cold pool.

Jump in damn it! Just take that icy first plunge, do a few laps, and pretty soon, you'll be used to it. A little pain, then you are in the gravy!

It's tough to jump into a new language too.

It's tough to jump into Spanish when you've just started learning it. You say a thing or two in class (you *have* to in class, they *called* on you), and you know that neighbor two doors down is from Peru, but... So you just stand there, with your linguistic ankle in the water.

Maybe you'll just wait here a little bit.

Maybe you'll wait until you're really good at it, or your accent's better, or your vocabulary's a little more robust, before you "take the plunge" and talk with your neighbor.

Jump in, damn it!

Just take that icy first linguistic plunge, say a few words, and pretty soon, you'll be used to it. Just like you got used to the cold water.

A common mistake of budding linguists is this "hesitation before the icy pool." You get all wrapped up in your ego ("What will they think of me? They'll think I'm stupid!") and hold off until you're "good enough."

Trouble is, "good enough" never happens.

If you're hesitant to jump in, you can always find a reason to "wait until I'm better." I've talked with people who are near-fluent in a language but they're reticent to speak:

"My accent is still poor."

"I always get mixed up with the plural."

"Maybe after my next class."

To hell with that thinking! You get *better* by getting out there and *trying*. If you throw yourself into it, flounder, mix up everything, fail to understand or to make yourself understood, SO WHAT? That failure is a stepping stone to the next time. At least you *pegged* what it is you need to know.

Example: You go down the street to talk with your Peruvian neighbor, bound and determined to talk about your kids.

"Mi hijo quiere (my son wants to…oops, you wanted to say, "My son wants to play baseball with your son", but you forgot how to say "play").

The neighbor says, "¿Tu hijo quiere que?" (Your son wants what?)

You imitate the motions of baseball. You've also forgotten how to say baseball.

"O! Tu hijo quiere jugar al beisbol!" (Oh, your son wants to play baseball!)

That's it! The Peruvian filled in for you. "Jugar al beisbol." That's what you were looking for.

So what's does this linguistic morality play tell us? You went down the street, you bucked up your courage, "jumped into the pool", shrugged off a slip-up, faked your message with sign language (a great way to "make do" when vocabulary fails), and got the message across anyway. Now you know how to say "play baseball", plus you've laid the foundation for more chit chats with your neighbor.

The alternative – stay in your house, keep working at your lessons or attending your classes until you're perfect, and you never talk with the neighbor. Wrongo!

Jump in! That's what you need to do.

Story to illustrate the point: (This pertains to French but the idea is the same).

1975, Saigon is falling. Helicopters are taking off from the roof of the American embassy; helicopters are getting thrown off the decks of our aircraft carriers. Panic everywhere.

A lot of the people leaving at that time were speakers of French, the "linguistic footprint" of the French colonial presence.

One of those families came to my hometown. I was precisely two weeks into a "Teach Yourself French" jag.

My Dad says, "Chris, those people have no one to speak with. Go over there and talk French to them."

"Um, Dad, I started learning French 2 weeks ago. I can only say, 'Hello, how are you.'"

"Good enough, I'll take you over there right now."

The sink-or-swim school of French!

Good point to remember, good idea to put into practice. Don't "wait until you're good", just get in there and start talking!

5. Just learn the "I" and "you" forms of verbs initially. They are the forms you will use the most.

In a perfect world, you have an infinite amount of time for language study.

Most of us lack that luxury.

-Work? Oh that. Bosses tend to pay you only when you show up and actually do something for that paycheck. Work tends to put a sizable divot in any language-study schedule.

-School? Same deal. Teachers only tend to pass you along to higher grades and eventually graduate you if you show up and do something for that report card. School tends to put a sizable divot in any language-study schedule as well.

-Family? Kids! Go figure. By the time you're done changing, feeding, pulling the AK-47 out of their curious little hands, you've burned up an entire day. No time left to memorize verbs or practice your numbers. (Some have suggested you wrap the kids in duct tape. By the time they unwrap themselves, you should be able to get a good 20 minute language lesson done. You could argue there is some element of cruelty and immorality to such a maneuver, but there's no arguing its efficacy!)

-Life in general. It has a tendency to happen. And it has a tendency to eat up your time.

What can you do about learning the most with the time limitations we all have?

When first learning a language, just learn the "I" and "you" forms of the verbs.

In almost any conversation you have at a beginning level, "I" and "you" will be the only people involved. So, since your time is limited, limit yourself to learning those two forms.

Yo hablo. (I speak)
Usted habla. (You speak)

Yo como. (I eat)
Usted come. (You eat)

Yo voy. (I go)
Usted va. (You go)

In language classes, they will always tell you *all* the forms for *all* the people. And that's great! You will *eventually* need those forms. But at the beginning, to get off the ground, to pound out your first few attempts at conversation, stick to two forms and two forms only. You're better off knowing the "I" and "you" forms of 50 verbs than knowing *all* the forms of 10 verbs. You just won't use the "we" and "they" forms as much.

To repeat, with infinite memory in your brain and infinite time on your hands, you should learn all the forms. But with limited memory (we're human) and limited time (ditto), we have to laser in on the things that will help us most.

So learn two forms, save the others for later.

6. Just learn the present and past of the verbs initially. Leave more complicated tenses for later.

Same argument here as in (5).

Do yourself the same favor you did before. Limit yourself, at the beginning, to learning those things you'll use *most* in conversation. And the two tenses you need are the present and the past.

Spanish has a bunch of different forms of the past, the two main ones being the preterite and the imperfect.

Preterite means an action that is completed.

"I ate a hamburger."
(Comí una hamburguesa.)

"Fuí a Neuva York."
(I went to New York.)

The imperfect is a little hazier. Don't worry about it for now. Just learn the preterite. Here are the ones you'll need.

Ser (To be)
Yo fuí – I was
Usted fué – You were

Ir (to go)
Fuí – I went
Fué – You went

Hey, what do you know, a freebie? The forms are the same! The "language Gods" do occasionally cut you some slack!

Querer (to want)
Quise – I wanted
Quiso – You wanted

Comer – (to eat)

Comí – I ate
Comió – You ate

Did you notice something? I'm not saying "yo" or "Usted" in front of these verbs. Turns out, you don't have to! The *form* of the verb "says who said it", so you can skip saying "Yo comí", and just say "Comí." Both mean "I ate." Truth to tell, saying "Yo comí" shows you're a beginner. No harm in that!

Later, as you get better, as you seek to understand the difference between "I was going" and "I went", then, by all means, take on the other tenses and forms. It will deepen your understanding and make you a better speaker. But right now we're talking about getting the initial baby steps down. And for that, learn the preterite (that will take care of the past just fine) and the present (that will take care of everything else for now).

7. "Slalom" through the different learning methods.

This hearkens back to the Magnificent Seven. As soon as you feel yourself bogging down, open a different book or pop a different CD in the player. As long as they're all teaching you Spanish, you can't go too far wrong.

8. All the time, keep that Spanish radio station on, keep that Spanish television station on (well, at least part of the time...) to keep improving your ear.

Sooner than you think, Spanish is going to start making sense. On the evening TV news, you used to only understand names –

Boosh (Bush), Pooteen (Putin), Pahrees Heeltone (our favorite celebrity).

But now you're starting to understand a few other words, picked up during your slalom runs. You start to understand a sentence or two during the TV news:

"Bush fué a Rusia para hablar con Putin." (Bush went to Russia to talk to Putin.)

The rest of the newscast goes over your head, but at least you understood that sentence.

It's important to keep listening, day in and day out. *Language* work is *volume* work. You don't have to be *brilliant*; you just have to be *dogged*. If you watch ten Spanish TV newscasts, you will learn more than if you watch two. The more the words wash over your ears, the more the words bathe your brain, the more will stick in your brain. That's how *kids* learn their first language. They hear Mom talking, day in and day out, and one day, the kid starts talking. Now, getting kids to shut up, that's the topic of another book!

On your way into work, the Spanish radio station will start to become understandable. Listen closely to the weather report.

You're driving in, windshield wipers slapping, barely able to see through the downpour. On the radio, they say, "Hoy, lluvia." (Today, rain.)

"No kidding", you mumble to yourself through gritted teeth as another 18-wheeler zooms past, blinding you with a gush of water. "'Hoy, lluvia'" is right." But at this point, you're not just memorizing a word for a word. This is no dictionary or classroom exercise. "Lluvia" is happening all over your car and the road. There is a *reality* to the word, an *emotional tag* on that damned lluvia that's making your commute a nightmare. You are starting to THINK in Spanish.

"Lluvia" doesn't have to go into your brain, get ground up and reconstituted as "rain", and then become something you understand. "Lluvia" is that wet stuff, that slippery stuff ready to hydroplane you into the ditch.

You'll never forget it now. You own "lluvia."

A few months later, listening to the weather report, the

broadcaster says, "Va a nevar" (it's going to snow) and just then, you see the first lacy, gossamer wings of approaching winter settle on your hood.

"Va a nevar" takes on that same reality, that same shortcut from Spanish words to an *actual thing*, rather than the long detour from Spanish words, to English words, to "oh, that's what it means."

These tiny breakthroughs, one raindrop and one snowflake at a time, are turning you into a linguist.

Turn on Univision and this time; sit through the whole half hour news broadcast. What do you know! A few more words make sense.

Now, a major cool thing is about to happen, call it the "tearing out the stamp effect." Here's how the analogy works. Think of stamps all together in one flat sheet. A square of 2 stamps across, 2 stamps down, making four stamps total.

1. To tear the first stamp out, you have to tear along *two* edges.
2. To take the second stamp and third stamp out, you just have to tear *one* edge.
3. To take the fourth stamp out, wait, it already IS out. You don't have to tear *anything*; it's already "free."

As you start to learn more Spanish, you are going to start getting some "freebees", just like you got a "freebee" with the last stamp. What do we mean by that?

- When you first learn Spanish, you have to fight to memorize each word in a sentence.

- Take the sentence, "Va a comenzar la semana que viene." (It's going to begin next week.) At the beginning, you had to learn what "va" meant, "a", "comenzar", everything. That's a lot of memorizing for a pretty simple sentence.

- But now you've been at it a while, and let's say you know everything but the word "comenzar" (to begin) in this sentence.

- So you say, "This sentence means 'It's going to _____ next week.'"

- Hmm. They were talking about the G-8 conference, a big meeting of all the economic powerhouses.

- Hey! "Comenzar" must mean "to start." They must have been talking about the meeting "starting" next week.

- Freebee! The "last stamp" fell out by itself. You were able to figure out what "comenzar" meant because you had all the rest of the sentence down, then you added a little common sense, and you got it!

The more you keep listening (and slaloming, like in number 7 above), the more Freebees you're going to get.

"El presidente de Honduras murió ayer."

You know that the president of Honduras did *something* yesterday. You know that because you know "El presidente de Honduras" and you know "ayer" (yesterday). But you don't know "murió."

Hey, his picture has black crepe hanging over it, there are two years listed, obviously that of his birth and his death. And that last year is *this* year. What else can it be? "Murió" must mean "died."

So, you learned a new word, and nobody had to teach it to you and you didn't need to look anything up. That fourth stamp was already freed up, no tearing needed!

Keep at it. Keep up that listening. Freebees will start falling in your lap like raindrops in April. Your ability to *receive* is improving by leaps and bounds.

But what about your ability to *send*? Remember, a language

is really two languages – a *sending* language and a *receiving* language.

9. Record yourself, listen to yourself, record yourself, listen to yourself.

Work on that sending skill! A few AAA batteries and your little Dictaphone and you're in business. Stuck for something to record? Read the little passage from your *Teach Yourself Spanish* book. Go to a Spanish language newspaper and read the day's lead article aloud into your Dictaphone.

Be ambitious; record a whole chapter from one of your side by side reading efforts.

Now that you have a whole chapter on tape (or on silica, whatever they hell they record with now in this digital world), go for your morning jog and listen to yourself recite the chapter. You've already read the book so you know the main things that happen, even if you don't remember all the details.

You spoke it; you read it, now you're hearing it.

You are "marinating your brain" in Spanish. Even if you always felt you were "bad at languages", you're bound to see some improvement as you keep at it.

Skill at language is not a question of brilliance; it is a question of persistence. When people ask me if I'm "good at languages", I say, "No, but I'm interested in them and I keep at them."

Good time for a side trip. Is there such a thing as being "incapable of learning a foreign language"? Aha! A true story answers that very question!

The Man Who Could Not Learn A Foreign Language

Many universities still have a foreign language requirement. Before you can graduate, you must take and pass a couple semesters of some language.

Enter a distant relative of mine who will remain nameless (but let's call him Bob).

Bob goes toe to toe with the university administration.

"I am incapable of learning a foreign language. I just can't do it."

To examine this contention, the University put together an ad hoc committee. (Presumably, they would have had to explain to Bob that "ad hoc" is a Latin term meaning "for a specific purpose").

They wrestled with the great questions of "linguistic-ness."

- No language is inherently harder to learn as a child than any other. All kids start speaking and master a language at about the same time, whether that is the four-toned Mandarin, guttural Arabic, clicking Xhosa, or the more familiar European languages.

- All kids get down the complexities of past, present, future, and "contrary to fact" sentences.

- Learning in adulthood is more complex. The Mormon Church, Armed Services, Diplomatic Service, and Peace Corps all have to train adults to speak a variety of tongues, and some languages just plain take longer than others. Spanish (thank goodness) is pretty easy for English speakers to learn, while Arabic and Chinese take twice as long to learn.

- Star Trek fans have even learned Klingon! Talk about a made-up, far-out language!

So it seems that Bob should be able to take a couple semesters of something without bursting his brains or anything.

But no! Enter science.

Bob produces a psychologist (in the pay and employ of Bob) who had done psychological tests that PROVED that he can't process a foreign language. The psychologist not only said Bob would be *bad* at languages, but that he is *mentally incapable* of learning them. He's the only person on the planet and in the history of mankind with such a handicap.

Science has spoken!

The University blinked. They made an exception for Bob, and he never had to take the language requirement.

End of story? Not quite.

Bob graduated, fell in love with an Italian woman, and moved to Italy. There, his diploma couldn't seem to land him a job, so he had to take up employment as a waiter.

A waiter.

In Italy.

Waiting on Italian people.

Guess what Bob had to learn to be able to survive.

Uh, Italian. The man, who had proven (to his school's satisfaction) that he could NOT EVER learn a language, became fluent in Italian.

I love that story.

And now, the last of our 10 Tips for slaying the Grammar Monster.

10. Cultivate friendships with Spanish speakers, go to Spanish festivals, and immerse yourself.

Immersion is the way to go. Just ask Bob.

If by chance you can do the real live immersion thing (Junior Year abroad, immersion language camp, go and live in Costa Rica for a year), do it! All the language courses and CD's and websites and classes in the world cannot compare to actually *picking up and going where they speak Spanish*.

Ask any Mormon who has done their two year mission abroad – you get a bunch of language teaching before you leave, but it doesn't compare to how much you learn once you are *there*.

When you're there, you HAVE to speak it. Bob reminds us of this important lesson.

So if you have the time/money/inclination, go for it.

What about the rest of us? Most people just can't do this. Too much money, too much time away from work or family, too much effort. But is there any kind of "half-way immersion" you can try?

Of course! Like everything else, it just takes a little detective work.

Spanish Heritage Festival in the next town? Go and spend half a day there. Walk around and keep your ear open and look for a chance to "strut your linguistic stuff." At least you can order some food in Spanish. While you're standing there watching some kids dance, ask the person next to you, "¿De donde es?" (Where are you from?) Pretty soon you'll strike up a conversation and before you know it, you'll have your own "mini-immersion."

Remember to say "Lo aprendí a mi mismo"!

Invite yourself over to the Venezuelan neighbor's for dinner? Aag! Can't be an oaf about this. But you can invite the Venezuelan to YOUR house for dinner. There it is another "mini-immersion" experience. Make every attempt to "stay in Spanish" the whole night. If you only make it through half the night, no problem. You got a "half-night of immersion." Better than no immersion at all.

Try to put yourself into a place where you can't "bail out" and use English as a crutch. Go to a festival where everyone is speaking Spanish, or invite a family over where no one speaks English. You'll be working like a dog all night, fumbling for the right word and the right phrase, and struggling to understand what they're saying.

But that's how you get better! You work at it!

Now you've tamed that grammar monster!

Next, we'll look at a language myth, "Why are Americans so bad at languages?" Or is it a myth?

Chapter 3

Why are Americans So Bad at Languages?

Why *are* Americans so bad at languages? Plenty of reasons (assuming, that is, that we really *are* so bad at languages, but I'll address that particular question a few paragraphs down), and some of them are wet.

Look at the globe, America has Mexico to our south (plenty of chances to learn Spanish there), Canada to our North (plenty of chances to learn French there, at least along the Quebec border, and two great big wet walls to our east and west. It's quite a leap from San Francisco Bay to Tokyo Bay, so no pressing need to learn Japanese there. And on the other end, you've got a few thousand miles between the harbor town of Baltimore and the harbor town of Lisbon in Portugal. So people in Maryland aren't mobbing the "Teach Yourself Portuguese" section of their local Barnes and Noble.

Contrast this with a little country in the middle of Europe, Luxembourg. Wedged between some big neighbors, the Luxembourgers HAVE to speak a few different languages, just to get around. A little west, and it's time to parler français (speak French), a few kilometers west, and you'd better put on your deutschsprechende Hut (German-speaking hat – of interest, all nouns in German are capitalized). Then, a half hour north, and everybody sprekt Nederlands (speaks Dutch).

Hardly anybody knows much about Luxembourg, so let's go down to Switzerland. Say you're a businessman selling widgets to nearby customers. Just south of you, you'll make your pitch in Italian. North of you, your power lunch will be conducted in German. To the west, you'll be closing deals in French. And on the off chance there's a dire shortage of widgets to your east, you'll be filling the gap in the dialect of tiny Lichtenstein! Egad.

What else makes Americans so one-languaged?

Boot up, click here, log on anywhere with your desktop, your laptop, or your hand held Internet-o-matic. What do you see? English.

No invading army forced English down the Internet's throat. No strutting tyrant lined people against the wall and shot them for creating non-English websites. No flying saucers circled Earth and used mind-control beams to create an English-speaking world wide web.

It just turned out that way.

Cyber land mostly speaks English.

So it's easy for Homo Americanus Monolingualicus to say, "Hey, why bother learning a foreign language? The world is computers, and computers speak English!" And it's not just computers that declare English the king of languages.

Show me the money.

When a Danish wholesaler of cheese goes into business with an Egyptian grocer, what is the go-between language? English.

At an international engineering meeting in Moscow, what language booms out at the Sheraton's main conference room? English.

Native art from Ghana goes on sale to collectors from New York, Paris and New Delhi. Does the auctioneer shout, "Going, going, gone!" in the French of Paris, the Hindi of New Delhi, or the Ewe of Ghana? No, he says "Going, going, gone", in the English of New York.

The dollar's getting pummeled lately by the euro, but that greenback of ours still dominates commerce around the world. That crisp 100 dollar Benjamin Franklin bill says, "This note is legal tender for all debts, public and private." It might just as well say, "And for all debts, national and international."

Those dollars insulate us linguistically just as much as those wide blue oceans.

Put it all together:

- Geography
- Internet
- Commerce.

And Americans are never *pushed* to learn another language. When you don't have to, why go through the effort? If you can get along fine in English, if you're not cheek-by-jowl with foreign speakers, if the Internet and the business world rarely demand knowledge of another lingo, it's the easiest thing in the world to "stay in English."

So what, should we collectively hang our heads in shame that we are so awful at languages?

Maybe not.

We may not be as *bad* as we're painted. This whole "Americans are terrible at languages" may well be a myth!

The Peri-Hispanic ribbon.

In a southern strip of America, from southern California across to Texas, then flying across the Gulf of Mexico and taking in southern Florida, America is bilingual. Americans handle two languages there quite nicely, thank you. Teachers, firefighters, emergency medical technicians, police, doctors, nurses – anyone who has contact with the community – all speak at least survival Spanish. A whole army of bilingual Americans attest to a command of language.

What about the *Army* army? The press is filled with reports that "we don't have enough linguists in the Army" – true enough. We don't have enough. But still, the Army does train a lot of linguists so we can "listen in" to the bad guys. One of the best places to learn a language (in case you should choose the Armed Forces for a career) is in the Army's language training center in Monterey, California.

Any other armies out there, training Americans to be

linguists? If you go to Utah and hook up with the Mormons, you'll see they have the language thing down to an art. Every year, the Mormons send out their young men on a two year mission to gain converts. Where do they go? Everywhere in the world. Before they go, their missionaries are trained in an intense immersion course. They, literally, cover the globe as far as languages are concerned. And once their mission is done – and after two years in wherever, they are *fluent* in that language – they now constitute a reservoir of language knowledge for future missions.

The Mormons are a slice of Americana that's pretty good with languages.

Check out the IMAX film *Mission to MIR.* The American astronauts that went aboard that old clunker of a space station all learned Russian before "going up." And Russian is pretty tough!

Pop into your local Border's or Barnes and Noble. An entire aisle of *Teach Yourself Spanish, Latin for Dummies, Chinese in 10 Minutes a Day, Pimsleur's Introductory Arabic,* and *Italian on the Go* greets you. According to the books and CD's on the shelves, Americans are indeed teaching themselves Cantonese and Dutch and Thai and Basque and you name it. We may not be the world's greatest linguists, but some of us seem to be *trying*.

The Ugly American saw publication decades ago. That classic book detailed the pushy, demanding American who has gone abroad. Among his other conceits, the ugly American required that all the world speak and understand English.

"Hey, where's the bus station? MISTER, YOU KNOW WHAT I'M SAYIN', WHERE THE HELL'S THE BUS STATION?"

"You *know* they know what I'm saying."

Does this beast still roam the earth, sowing resent and contempt in his wake?

Well, yes, no doubt, that still goes on. But the ugly American is yielding to a "kinder, gentler" traveler. In my own experience, I've seen a lot of my fellow American paisanos making quite the effort to learn the lingo:

- In Ecuador, during a medical mission with Interplast, all the doctors and nurses on the trip learned the "survival Spanish" they needed. Surgeons learned the names of the instruments, nurses learned the phrases necessary for the recovery room.

- In Norway, the American tourists at nearby tables always thanked the waiters with "Tak" (Thanks, in Norwegian). That might not be a fluent dissertation on ancient Viking tales, but it's an effort.

- In France, Italy, Portugal, Spain, and Denmark – anywhere you go – you'll see Americans shedding the bad guy, English-only image. People from Chicago, Atlanta, LA, Kansas City, are "treading lightly" when they go out into the world, not forcing everything into the American image, or the American lingo. They are reaching out to connect with the locals, and connect with them in the local language.

Corny as this may sound, it makes me proud to see Americans making that leap. It takes a lot of work to learn a foreign language!

Ambassadors all, those hard-studying, foreign-speaking Americans. Ambassadors of good will at a time when the USA could *use* a little more good will.

Let's take another look at the idea that "All Americans are *bad* at languages; all Europeans are *great* at languages. Europeans all speak 3 or 4, you know."

Closer inspection shows that the first half of that sentence is not true. There *are* some Americans good at languages.

How about the second half? Do "All Europeans speak 3 or 4 languages"?

You might be surprised at how great the Europeans *aren't*.

Yes, the Frenchman at the border of Italy will, by dint of travel and work, pick up Italian. And the German who works with Polish border authorities will speak Polish because his job requires it and he practices it all the time. At international medical meetings, the Europeans you meet will all have a great command of English. They have to, since that is the language most meetings are held in.

But not everyone does international work and cross-cultural exchanges on a regular basis. Europe, like America, has all kinds of homebodies who stick close to home, are perfectly comfortable in their native tongue, and don't bother learning or retaining anything else.

No crime there.

A Swede may learn English at school, then get a job close to home, and over time, he forgets his English. Same for an Austrian or Spaniard or Romanian or Dane.

On *average*, you will find more linguists in Europe, no doubt. But there is no need for us to bow and scrape before the almighty, all-knowledgeable, all-speak-four-languages Europeans. It just ain't so. A lot of them are just like us. One language and one language alone.

So when you add it all up, will geography, computers, and dollars all conspire to make us a land of mono-linguists?

Maybe the opposite!

As globalizations melts borders (where does *Microsoftia* end and *International Monetary Fundia* begin?), as hand-held computer/cell phone/Internet access/video cameras link us from Tierra del Fuego to Ulaan Bator, and as free market dollars fly around the globe, we might just get *better* at languages.

- As long as you're e-mailing your friend in Shanghai, might as well download a pod cast on *Teach Yourself Cantonese* and learn a few phrases.

- Business people of all stripes will be doing work all over the place. Seal the deal in the customers' language? Not a bad idea.

- Web sites all over the place can help with language instruction or brushing up. The BBC, for example, and Swedish radio both have the news in dozens of languages. And they broadcast in those languages too, so you can "tune your ear" to the sound of the target language of your choice. No more tuning in a shortwave radio late at night, hoping some feeble signal from Paris will bounce off the atmosphere and make it to your antenna.

- Learning companies are "heeding the call" for better language instruction, so there are zillions of grammar books, phrasebooks, interactive CD's and DVD's (*Pimsleur* is great for listening, *Rosetta Stone* is great for watching).

The future's so bright, you almost have to wear shades, as the song says!

But we've gotten off track; let's get back to learning Spanish. Some of this will be review (always good), and some of it will push us a little deeper into Spanish. You'll notice ideas from "The Magnificent Seven" popping up every now and then.

We'll start out with a review of the big phrases, and then we'll go wrestle with a little more grammar.

THE PHRASES THAT OPEN THE MOST DOORS

Let's go over this again.

How do you say that in Spanish? — *¿Como se dice eso en español?*

What does that mean? — ¿Que quiere decir eso?

Use this when you're pointing to something and you have blanked on the above phrases:

What is that? — ¿Que es eso?

With these, you can manage almost anything. Listen carefully to what the Spanish speaker says, and then repeat what they said out loud. Always repeat what they say! That locks it into your memory, and it allows them to correct you if you said it wrong. (This point is worth repeating!)

Example:
You're in front of a shoe store and you forgot how to say "shoe." You're with a friend from Mexico.
You point to the shoe in the display window.
"¿Come se dice eso en español?"
"Zapato."
"¿Gazpacho?"
"No, no", (your friend laughs at you – get used to it, budding linguists get laughed at a lot). "Zapato. Za – pa – to."
"Zapato."
"Sí, zapato."
You've got it.

VERBS

Since you're a little further along, and ready to go more in depth, we'll go ahead now and show you all the forms of the verbs. Recall from the earlier chapter, I put most of your energy into the "I" and "you" forms of the verbs as those are the ones you'll use the most.

First, something you should know about how to say "you" in Spanish.
Spanish has two forms for "you", the "tu" form (familiar, informal) and the "Usted" form (formal). In the early going,

stick with the Usted form, since it's better to be too formal than too presumptuous. Once you get to know a person well, or if you're talking with children, then you can use the "tu" form. These forms of you have different verb forms (or conjugations, as these different forms are called). You'll see these different forms as we go through the verbs below.

Spanish has two main forms of the past tense, the preterite and the imperfect. (Earlier, we just learned the preterite. Now we'll include the imperfect.)

To understand the difference, we're going to raft down the Niagara River with a zoned out pothead wearing headphones whose music drowns out the sound of the impeding falls.

This misguided person gets into the Niagara River and takes a long, clueless float down the river. Hour after hour he's floating along, ignoring the quickening current and unable to hear the roar of approaching disaster. Finally, it happens, he plunges over the falls and is killed on the rocks below.

"Flotaba sobre el superficie del río, entonces cayo y murió."

(He was floating [flotaba – the imperfect form] on the surface of the river, and then he fell and died [cayó y murió – the preterite form]).

The imperfect form describes a past tense that was ongoing.

The preterite form describes a one-time, completed action.

Flotaba – (he was floating) has the notion that this poorly advised fellow was just lazing along the river, hour after hour passes and he just keeps floating along. Just like the imperfect tense just keeps floating and floating along.

Cayó y murió – (he fell and died) is boom! Done! Over and done with!

This verb form has a definite start and stop. The preterite is a completed action.

To always get the imperfect/preterite tense nailed down correctly is impossible. That's the bad news. What's the good news? Like everything else in "Grammar World", a mistake does not mean you're incomprehensible. If you say an imperfect when you should say a preterite or vice versa, it's not a great big deal. OK, sometimes they might have a little trouble understanding you, but it's no different than when a Spanish speaker makes a grammar mistake in English. We usually understand them.

Here are some examples of these different forms.
Preterite of flotar (to float):
Yo floté (I floated)
Tu flotaste (You – familiar – floated)
El, ella flotó (He, she, floated)
Nosotros flotamos (We floated)
Usted flotó (You – formal – floated)
Ellos flotaron (They floated)

Imperfect of flotar:
Yo flotaba (I was floating, used to float – the idea of no specific one time)
Tu flotabas (You – familiar – were floating)
El, ella flotaba (He, she was floating)
Nosotros flotábamos (We were floating)
Usted flotaba (You – formal – were floating)
Ellos flotaban (They were floating)

This is where the book *201 Spanish Verbs* comes in handy. You go to a bunch of verbs you'll want to use:
-comer – to eat
-hablar – to speak
-ir – to go
-jugar – to play
-oir – to listen
Now write down the preterite and imperfect forms of these verbs, maybe write the "I" and "you" forms in capital letters.

After you've written a few, the "rule" for making the preterite will become clear.

Preterite endings are:
-é
-aste
-ó
-amos
-ó
-aron

But this is just for verbs that end in –ar. For verbs that end in –ir or –er, the endings are:
-í
-iste
-ió
-imos
-ió
-ieron

Preterite forms are peppered with irregularities. And, in a maddening twist, most of the irregularities are in the most commonly used verbs! Aaag! OK, so no one said this would be a cake walk.

Now let's go on to the other form, the imperfect:

Imperfect endings for –ar verbs are:
-aba
-abas
-aba
-ábamos
-aba
-aban

For –ir and –er verbs:
-ía
-ías

-ía
-íamos
-ía
-ían

Imperfect forms have far fewer irregularities. Much less of a pain to get these forms down. At times, when the preterites are just not jumping into your brain, you may find yourself "bailing out" and going to the "easier to manage" imperfect forms. Better this than "bailing out" into English! Try to stay in Spanish!

The two forms of "to be."

What's with all these "two forms of"? Two forms of "you", two forms of the past, and now two forms of "to be." Hey! That's how it goes with languages. They seem foreign sometimes, surprise surprise.

Ser means "to be" in a permanent sense.

Estar means "to be" in a less permanent sense.

And boy howdy there are some exceptions!

Forms of "ser"
Yo soy (I am)
Tu eres (you – familiar – are)
El, ella, es (he, she, it – is)
Nosotros somos (we are)
Usted es (you – formal – are)
Ellos son (they are)

Forms of "estar"
Yo estoy
Tu estas
El, ella esta
Nosotros estamos
Usted está
Ellos estan

So, you say "Yo soy americano." (I am American.) because that is a permanent state. But you say "Yo estoy en el teatro ahora mismo." (I am in the theater right now.) because this is a temporary state. You'll be out of the theater in a few hours and going back home.

Spanish has a lot more tenses (so do we).
Future tense – I will eat breakfast at Tiffany's.
Conditional tense – I would eat breakfast at Tiffany's.
Perfect tense – I have or had eaten breakfast at Tiffany's.
Subjunctive – I prefer that he eat breakfast at Tiffany's.
Future perfect – By this time tomorrow, I will have eaten breakfast at Tiffany's.

Spanish has forms for all these!
My advice? Stick with the present and the two past forms. Ignore the subjunctive until you are WAY into the language. If you're speaking well enough that the subjunctive is making a difference, then you're already damned near fluent anyway.

To "fake" the future, you can always use the form of "ir" (to go) plus the infinitive form of the verb.

In case you forgot, the infinitive is the "to ___" form of the verb. Here are some Spanish infinitives and their English equivalents:
Ir – to go
Aprender – to learn
Interesar – to interest

So here goes with the cheap and easy form of the future:

Yo voy a comer. (I am going to eat – just like we say in English for the future!)
Tu vas a salir. (You are going to leave.)
El va a conducir. (He is going to drive.)
Nosotros vamos a almorzar. (We are going to eat breakfast.)
Usted va a escribir. (You are going to write.)
Ellos van a llegar. (They are going to arrive.)

Now you've got a future form in your quiver.

How about all the other forms? No kidding, hold off on them for a while. You'll do better to pound down a lot of these simpler, more-often-used forms (present, past, the occasional future). You're early in the going still, and unlikely to say a lot of sentences with "would" or "I prefer that" in them. You're a lot closer to fluency with a bunch of common verbs and common tenses that you can *use*, rather than a litany of tougher, less-often-used tenses and shades of meaning that rarely enter beginning conversations.

PRONOUNS

These little words are easy to trip over. It's easy to get gummed up in the grammar-ese too, with talk of intransitive this and reflexive that and indirect versus direct. This is when "grammar" starts to earn its bad name. So let's try to keep it light so we don't get all freaked out.

The regular old pronouns:
I – yo
You (familiar) – tu
He – él
She – ella
You (formal) – Usted
We – nosotros
They – ellos

Not so bad. Here's a point brought up earlier - you most often omit the pronoun. For example, "hablamos" means "we speak." The form of the verb *says* who is speaking. So, unlike English, where we always have to say the pronoun, the Spanish speakers don't have to. Just say the verb.

At the beginning, you will still say the pronoun, because it "reassures you" and "sounds right." No problem! Saying an extra word or two isn't a problem.

The pronouns when they're *not* regular old pronouns.
Here's where it gets tough.
Me – me or mi
You (familiar) – te or ti
He – le or lo
She – le or la
You (formal) – le or lo
Us – nos
Them – les or los

The first forms are when the pronouns are a DIRECT object.

If I say, "I shot Sheriff John Brown in the head", then Sheriff John Brown was the direct recipient of my Colt .45. That makes him about as DIRECT (and dead) an object as you can imagine.

If, instead, I give something TO Sheriff John Brown, then that makes him an INDIRECT object. "I handed a lit stick of TNT to Sheriff John Brown."

The Sheriff is having a bad day!

In this sentence, the lit stick of TNT is the DIRECT object, and the doomed Sheriff John Brown is the INDIRECT recipient of my action.

Now, when you first start talking Spanish, it is damned difficult, as you're making up sentences, to "see" the pronouns coming, and harder still to make sure you swerve to the direct one, then swerve to the indirect one, as you are talking along. To top it off, Spanish puts direct and indirect pronouns in front of the verbs!

I you see. (Yo te veo.)
I him give the book. (Yo le doy el libro.)

Ay caramba, this is the formula for a linguistic shipwreck!

Reason to despair?

Never! The linguist never despairs. The linguist always goes back to the prime directive – JUST PLOW AHEAD AND DO THE BEST YOU CAN. IF YOU MAKE A MISTAKE IN THE PRONOUNS, THEY'LL STILL UNDERSTAND YOU.

Better to push yourself and go for some complicated sentences, even if your understanding of the pronouns is a little shaky. All this comes with usage. Push in, push in, and keep pushing into the language. Make those mistakes, and just grind right over them and keep going.

AGREEMENT OF NOUNS AND ADJECTIVES

Spanish, unlike English, has masculine and feminine nouns.

La casa – the house, feminine. Most feminines end in "a", with some exceptions.

El gato – the cat, masculine. Most masculines end in "o", with some exceptions. Damned languages, always with the exceptions!

Adjectives come after the noun (most of the time) and have to agree with the noun.

La casa blanca – the white house. El gato blanco – the white cat.

And the adjectives have to agree in number as well.

Las casas blancas – the white houses. Los gatos blancos – the white cats.

Note that the words for "the" change as well. For feminine, the words are "la" and "las." For masculine, the words are "el" and "los."

GRAMMAR WRAP UP

No, that can't be it for grammar. Can it? There's a ton more grammar!

True, there is more grammar. But this is the grammar you need to *get going*. This is the grammar that will allow you to smash into your language books, your *Pimsleur* listening course, your *Rosetta Stone* computer course, your first few conversations, and your dual-reading exercises.

Don't get hung up on *every aspect of grammar* this early on – it'll get tedious and your all-important drive will start to wane. Just focus on this stuff:

-Opening phrases – Know "How do you say X?" and "What does X mean?"

-Verbs – present and the two pasts.

-Pronouns – don't sweat it if you mix up indirect and direct.

-Agreement of nouns and adjectives.

If you have these elements down, and you start laying in a good vocabulary on top of it, you're on your way to fluency. You'll know when it's time to add a new verb tense to your repertoire. That alone will tell you you're making progress.

There you have it, grammar in a nutshell. Wasn't that bad, was it?

Let's wrap up this intro chapter with a list of what you need to know to get along in Spanish. Not the impossible, "You need to speak 2,000 words to communicate." that you'll hear thrown around. This is a more manageable "100 or so words that will launch you." Remember, you just need enough to get out there and start mixing it up with the Spanish speakers. Here goes:

Yes. Sí.
No. No.
Perhaps. Talvez.

Buenos días. Good morning.
Buenas tardes. Good afternoon.

Buenas noches. Good evening.

¿Como esta? How are you?
Muy bien, gracias. Very well, thanks.

Me llamo *X*. My name is *X*.
¿Como se llama? What is your name?

¿Que es esto? ¿Que es eso? What is this? What is that?
Gracias. Thanks.
Por favor. Please.
De nada. You're welcome.

Yo doy. I give
Usted da. You give.

Yo hablo. I speak.
Usted habla. You speak.

Yo entiendo. I understand.
Usted entiende. You understand.

Yo como. I eat.
Usted come. You eat.

Yo voy. I go.
Usted va. You go.

Yo soy. I am. (Permanent state)
Usted es. You are.

Yo estoy. I am. (Temporary state)
Usted esta. You are

Mucho gusto. Nice to meet you.
Hasta luego. See you later.

Soy de Chicago. I'm from Chicago.
¿De donde es? Where are you from?

Repite, por favor. Please repeat.
Hable mas despacio. Speak more slowly.

¿Come se dice *X* en español? How do you say *X* in Spanish?
¿Que quiere decir esto? What does this mean?

¿Donde estan los servicios? Where's the restroom?
Una cerveza, por favor. A beer please.
Tequila, por favor, me hace hablar con mas fluidez.
Tequila, please, it makes me speak more fluently.

So we started this chapter examining this statement: "Americans are bad at languages."

Myth? Truth? At least we know this – YOU are going to be good at languages.

Chapter 4

"I Took Spanish for 3 Years and I Can't Say a Thing."

Here's another one we've all heard. It ranks right up there with "All Americans are bad at languages." So let's look at this one and see if we can turn it into our favor. Let's look at how languages are usually taught, then let's look at how they *should* be taught, and let's wrap it all up with a good Spanish lesson. As before, you'll see "The Magnificent Seven" peeking out here and there.

Language classes have three big problems:

1. **Emphasis on the written, not the spoken.**
2. **Not enough individual attention.**
3. **Summer forgetting.**

Disclaimer: Language study through classroom work has a long track record and a million success stories. The following focuses on those aspects of classroom language study that have misfired for lots of students. I'm not saying "Don't take language classes." I am saying, "You can often do as well or better on your own."

Emphasis on the written, not the spoken.

A teacher in any school setting faces a whirlwind of red tape. And the most troublesome part of that snarl is the need to grade. Some students will get A's, some B's, and so on. What a student actually learns and can use may take a backseat to the school administrator's demand for a "grade list." And the best way to hammer out those curves and crank out those grades?

- Written tests.
- Written assignments.

- Out comes the red pen, out flow the check marks, up go the grading curves, into the office fly the grades.

So, education has happened, right?

All grand and all perfect, the only problem is, that has very little bearing on the experience of speaking languages.

We speak with our mouths, and only secondarily do we communicate with our pens and papers. The *written* stands as great adjunct to learning a language, but we don't hand notes to people on the streets of Mexico City or Madrid.

We speak. We listen to the spoken word. We use our mouths, and we use our ears.

And grading? Doesn't exist.

When you speak and listen, you might make a hundred mistakes, but you keep working it until you make yourself understood and until you understand what the other people are saying. No one takes out a red pen and makes a mark in the air when you use the wrong tense, or when you garble the singular and plural, or when you forget to make the adjective agree with the noun.

As long as you get your message across, no matter how many "mistakes", you just got yourself an A+ in the "report card of the real world."

Some teachers do great oral exercises and work up conversational skills in their classes. Glory hallelujah and all the more power to them! Would that there were more of them.

But, fact is, most classes work on the written, give homework in the written, test the written, live and die by the written. And that leaves all too many language students with the lament "I studied for years, but when I went there, I couldn't understand a thing. I couldn't pick up what anyone was saying, and I totally blanked on saying anything myself."

The students' brains were wired for written skills, not oral skills.

They were wired to pass tests and get grades; they weren't

wired to go out there and mix it up in the rough and tumble world of conversation!

Reason to despair?

Never!

The die-hard linguist never despairs. The die-hard linguist just keeps working at it until he or she gets it. Never give up.

Let's analyze this problem of the written/spoken and come up with a better way.

If you're going to go out onto the street and talk to people having to do all the work in their language, you have to learn *two* languages, not just one. (This hearkens back to the recordings you did on your Dictaphone.)

*"What? It's hard enough to learn **one** language, now you're telling me I have to learn **two**?"*

Language is like a two-way walkie-talkie. There's one button for receiving – that's when you listen to the foreign language and understand what's coming *in*. And there's another button for sending – that's when you formulate the thought, put it into the other language yourself, and send it *out* in intelligible fashion. They are two distinct skills, and at various times you will find yourself better at one or the other.

Receiving – You have the advantage of not having to put together the syntax or grammar. The native speaker has done that for you. Their grammar is perfect, as is their pronunciation.

You have the *disadvantage* of *not knowing what's coming*. They might be talking about the weather, the upcoming election, the price of gold, or the fact that you are stepping on their foot.

Sending – You have the advantage of knowing what's coming. In your head, you have picked the topic, and you know what you want to say.

You have the *disadvantage* of– *finding* the vocabulary, *wrestling* with the syntax and grammar, and finally *coughing the words out* in something vaguely resembling the sounds of the native speakers.

Two distinct tasks!

Receiving – Spoken language does not provide convenient spaces like written language does. So the first time you hear someone speaking, let's say, Spanish, it sounds like this:

Allthewordsruntogetherinabigjumbleandyoucan'tpickoutth ewordsatall…itjustseemslikeonegiganticword…allruntogether.

In Spanish, for example, the simple phrase, "Nice to meet you," looks easy enough in the written form.

Mucho gusto en conocerle.

But when someone speaks it to you, especially quickly, it comes across like this to your ear:

Muchogustoenconocerle.

So it's your task to somehow break that word into intelligible chunks and digest it. (Don't worry, I'll tell you how.)

Sending – Now you turn it around. You're the one who's going to do the talking. Ah, what a relief, no surprises. I know exactly what I want to say.

But wait, that means *I* have to do the work of stuffing my English ideas into foreign packaging. I'm relieved of the burden of plucking those jumbled-together words apart. But I'm saddled with all the *creative* effort.

How do you say, "Nice to meet you."? If you haven't memorized the phrase itself, you're left with having to create it from scratch.

Let's see, "nice" is "simpático."

"To" is "para."

"Meet" is, oh hell, I forgot the word!

"You" is "Usted."

So, to send this message, I'm left with "Simpatico para (something) Usted."

This is one message that I can't send!

So, as we try to escape from the artificial world of written Spanish (as learned in classes) to the real world of spoken Spanish, we see we have two different dragons to slay.

Dragon number one: Picking the meaning out of a jumble of words flying past us.

Dragon number two: Formulating our ideas into meaningful phrases.

It really is *two different languages*.

So what do you do?

Receiving:

Immerse yourself in the sounds of the language right away. Doesn't matter that you don't know what they're saying, just start "hearing" right away. Let's look at Spanish, since that's our "target" and it's so useful to know Spanish.

At home, turn on a Spanish speaking channel. Watch the news – there's always a picture of what they're talking about so you'll at least have an idea of what's going on. You'll find you can at least pick out a few things, such as "American" words pronounced in the "Spanish" way.

- There's a picture of President Bush and pictures of combat in Iraq. You hear what sounds like "Boosh" (that's how they pronounce Bush) and you hear "Eerahk" (that's how they pronounce Iraq).

- A big flood in China is washing away houses. You hear "Cheena." Guess what, that's how they pronounce China. They keep showing houses being washed away and you keep hearing "casas." Well, you just picked up how they say "houses." Oh, and you remember that "flood" is "inondación" (remember when you saw the "Inondación en Bangladesh"?)

- The election is heating up and Hillary Clinton

keeps appearing. You hear "Cleentone", but you don't understand anything else. Doesn't matter, your "receiving" skill is growing.

Pick up a *Teach Yourself Spanish* CD and listen to it in the car. The *Pimsleur* series works well and requires no "reading along." This is good, because reading while you're driving can be hazardous to your health!

At home on your computer, use an interactive CD (the *Rosetta Stone* series is well designed and extremely effective). This does allow you to read along.

Listen in whenever and wherever you hear people speaking Spanish.

The idea here is simple – the more you expose your ear to the sound of Spanish, the better. A magic moment will arrive when that absolutelyunintelligiblestringofsounds suddenly seems to separate out into words you can understand.

The various learning tapes, CD's, TV shows, pod casts, DVD, and computer programs all *complement* each other. Don't rely on any *one* method. Use all the different methods to bathe your ears in the sound of Spanish. Even if you can't focus your attention on it, even if it's just background sounds as you work around the house or office, it's good to have it there, sneaking into your brain.

Sending:

The more you talk, the better. Fortunately, the Bluetooth thingies you put in your ear now "allow" you to walk around, talking to yourself, without people considering you insane. Good option.

A lot of teaching programs provide spaces after they say a phrase for you. Take advantage of it, speak up! Worried about making a mistake or sounding stupid? Time to learn the PRIME LESSON OF LANGUAGE LEARNING.

DON'T WORRY ABOUT MAKING MISTAKES. JUMP RIGHT IN AND SWING FOR THE FENCES.

A good linguist makes a thousand mistakes.
A great linguist makes ten thousand mistakes.
The world's greatest linguists make a million mistakes.

This is where "learning a language so you can really speak it" differs from "classroom learning" at the most fundamental level.

If you want to master Spanish, you wade right in and speak away, making mistakes left and right, but steadily overcoming the mistakes, picking up vocabulary, building confidence, and eventually making Spanish your second language.

If you want to "get a good grade in Spanish class", you tiptoe in, sticking only to what you learned in the previous lesson, learning only what you were told to learn, and hugging "the familiar" so you get all the questions right on the test and you get an "A."

SPEAKING A LANGUAGE IS NOT ABOUT STICKING TO WHAT YOU KNOW AND GETTING A GRADE. SPEAKING A LANGUAGE IS ABOUT PUSHING THE ENVELOPE EVERY DAY AND BORING DEEPER AND DEEPER INTO THE LANGUAGE.

As you push forward you'll conjugate verbs wrong, mix up genders, mangle word order, and get a lot of blank stares from people who don't understand you. Your way will be strewn with mistakes and errors and glitches and screw-ups and rough patches where you say, "I'll never learn Spanish, it's too tough!" and you'll want to give up.

But you won't, because you are a linguist, and a linguist knows that this is how it happens. Learning a language is like laying siege to a strong castle, and you'll have to batter against those walls again and again before you even see the first crack.

But you will see that crack.

It might be the first time you have a three word conversation with a Mexican you meet at work. It might be the third day on your *Rosetta Stone* program where you find yourself able to express yourself. It might be the first time you have Univision on your TV and you understand half of what they're saying in a story about a bank robbery.

But you will see that crack, and that means the castle will eventually fall, if you keep at it.

Keep battering, keep speaking aloud, keep at it. The castle will fall.

Don't sweat the mistakes, just keep plowing ahead.

Way back at the beginning of this chapter, we looked at the three big problems that afflict classroom learning. To review, they were:

1. **Emphasis on the written, not the spoken.**
2. **Not enough individual attention.**
3. **Summer forgetting.**

We've addressed the first problem, emphasis on the written, not spoken. By working at improving our receiving and our sending, we're now overcoming that first problem.

What about the second problem, not enough individual attention?

In a classroom, you're sitting there, waving your arm around, trying to get the teacher's attention. The teacher of your Spanish class just asked, "Who knows how to say, 'Good night'?"

You know, you say, "Buenas noches."

The teacher scans around the room, you've already answered a bunch of times and the idea is to "involve" everyone.

"Anyone? Tom? How about you?"

Nothing.

Your hand is waving, you're starting to support the "up"

hand with your other hand.

"Dick? Do you know?"

Nothing.

"Harry?"

Tom, Dick, and Harry all know nothing and say nothing. And you are sitting there, going out of your mind, dislocating your shoulder trying to get the teacher's attention.

Finally the teacher says, "Buenas noches. That's how you say it."

Your arm collapses. You collapse.

For better or worse, this is the curse of the classroom. Fine if you're just trying to get by, get along, and get a decent grade. But NOT fine if you are a linguist, intent on actually learning a language. There's too much time making sure "everyone participates", when what you want is individual attention so YOU can nail this language down.

In grade school, high school, college, adult learning classes, it always ends up this way. The teacher, just by the way school is structured, ends up "catering to the slowest." Nothing inherently wrong with that, and that's what teachers have to do. But you are not here to be the Mother Teresa of your time, sharing your precious time with the masses so "they can be helped too." You're here to learn Spanish, period!

When you teach *yourself*, when you *take command* of your own learning, you get *all the individual attention you need*. You study *when* you want, *where* you want, *how* you want, and *how much* you want.

Working with *Rosetta Stone*? Great program. Their proponents claim, "It's like having your own teacher talking to you." And it is! If you're not getting something, if the pronunciation is pretty rough, you can go over it as many times as you want. If you're getting it and want to move along at a faster clip, you can do that to.

No catering to "the classroom at large"; you are "catering to you."

Here's a great learning tip to give yourself all the individual attention you could possibly want. This will also help you review grammar and vocabulary painlessly.

The Grammar Wall.

You're far enough into a language that you know how to say things, can manage a few phrases, have read *El Principito*, but your desire to understand kicks in.

"How do you say the past tense?"

"Why do they put the pronouns where they do?"

"Why are the adjectives different for different words?"

It's great to be able to say stuff, but we are born *solvers*. (Note how popular crossword puzzles and Sudoku are, they both require solving a riddle.) We want to know *how* something is put together. When you reach that point in your language study, when you reach that Grammar Wall (grammar is no more or less then telling you the *how* the language is put together), then you do your next step in your studies.

Pick up the *Teach Yourself Spanish* book (any one will do, *Berlitz, Cortina, Teach Yourself* series) and look at the grammar sections.

Aha! You see that the adjectives match the nouns in gender and number. And in Spanish, the adjectives come after the nouns. OK, that's why the side-by-side book said:

Estrellas frías — Cold stars

You are teaching yourself Spanish, you are giving yourself all the attention you can handle, you are not waiting for other people in the class, and you have even taken on that awful demon **GRAMMAR** and seen that it's not so bad as it's painted.

Grammar helps you understand how they put the language together. It's the skeleton underlying and holding up the living body of the language. So, since you are now a linguist (not just a student suffering through class), you actually seek out this grammar, so you can better work the language.

Once again, you are slaying the Grammar Monster.

Now, grammar can be pretty dusty, I'm the first to admit it. So don't try to swallow it all at once. Go back to your pleasant reading of the side-by-side books. Pick up where Harry Potter left off, and read about his latest adventure. Or start in again where Agatha Christie was just about to explain how "the butler did it."

At another point, you'll hit another Grammar Wall. At another point, you'll wonder, "Well, just how do you say the past tense?" So, back to the grammar book.

Back and forth you go, getting all the individual attention you could want. Read along, jump to the grammar to clear up a point or two, go back to the books. Back and forth, one helping the other. The more grammar you pick up, the more sense the book makes. The more of the book you read, the more of the grammar that will start to "sink in."

Hey, as long as you have that Dictaphone around, add this to the mix. Read a chapter of Harry Potter into the Dictaphone. Then later, when you're out for a walk in the park, listen to it as you walk. Do you understand some? Even a little?

Give yourself all the individual attention you need until you do.

What are the problems with classroom language learning again?

1. **Emphasis on the written, not the spoken.**
2. **Not enough individual attention.**
3. **Summer forgetting.**

We've wrestled with numbers (1) and (2). What do we do about (3), the problem of summer forgetting?

Summer forgetting is a symptom of being a classroom student. (Summer forgetting never happens if you adopt the "24/7" of the Magnificent Seven.)

"Hey, it's June 5, summer vacation starts today! Throw out the books, forget homework, let's party all summer!"

Three months later, September heaves into view, and the first day of ignore-for-three-months Spanish class comes along, and you've forgotten everything. You spend September and October just getting to where you were last May and June.

Solution?

The linguist never takes summer vacation, because you are not "painted into a corner" by classroom schedules. You're not taking a class that meets at such and such a time in such and such a place. You are actively teaching yourself as you go along:

- You're reading *The Seven Habits of Highly Effective People* in English with the Spanish version alongside.

- In your car, you have a Spanish language station on when you go to pick up the kids.

- Turns out the neighbors three doors down are from the Dominican Republic, so you go out of your way to talk with them in Spanish when you run into them.

- At work, you have a *Rosetta Stone* CD set, and you get into work 15 minutes early to do a little reviewing before the work day ramps up.

There is no "summer vacation" from self-learning. You keep at it.

That's not to say you don't ease off every now and then. We're human, sometimes you do need a break. Work gets brutal, the home front gets a little brittle, a big project is coming up – life happens, as it tends to do. You notice, "Ooops, been a little while since I've reviewed my Spanish."

Don't sweat it. It will come back that much quicker if you've "learned it once." A few slides and a few stutters pop up in any language pursuit. Not the end of the world. Just hop back on the

Spanish express, fill in what you forgot, and keep going.

You must have worked up an appetite by now. Let's go eat an elephant.

Chapter 5

Eating an Elephant

"You can eat an entire elephant, provided you do it one forkful at a time. And you are patient."

A quote from somewhere, just can't remember where.

Time to start pounding on the Spanish. Time to sit down and start devouring that whole damned elephant of a language.

Get your fork.

To become really fluent, you need a couple thousand words under your belt. That's a pretty tall order.

We've already learned my cheap tricks for getting started in Spanish. Let's review them:

- Learn a few crucial phrases.
- Learn the "I" and "you" forms.
- Learn the present and one past form.
- Jump in with both feet and start talking.

So far, we can manage that. But a couple thousand words, come on! How are we going to do that?

Fear not, there is a way. It's going to be some work and take some time, but it's worth it. Here's a cliché to keep your nose to the grindstone.

Nothing worthwhile is easy.

Becoming fluent is worthwhile, so it's not going to be easy. But keep repeating the mantra about the elephant. You *can* eat the whole thing, as long as you stick to *one forkful at a time* and as long as you are *patient*. We'll tackle this three ways:

1. **Overall game plan.**
2. **Attack on vocabulary.**
3. **Attack on grammar. (There's no getting around that grammar monster!)**

Game plan.

Learn a little every day. Don't push yourself to absorb a huge amount of material in a day. First, you won't remember much. Second, this turns Spanish study into a grind and a bore. Pretty soon you'll resent Spanish!

"Damnation! I ate up my entire Saturday on a bunch of stupid verbs."

This is the **death** of your language pursuit. As soon as you resent Spanish, it's over. All the books, tapes, CD's, DVD's, websites – all for naught – if your will to learn is sapped. Your **desire** and **enthusiasm** are the most important components of learning Spanish. All else hinges on that! A million dollars of superb learning material does nothing for you if your heart's not in it.

So, early on, figure out what works for you. How much can you do every day, and not feel imposed upon? You don't need to go crazy on this (like I did), the most important thing is to find a little time, here and there, and keep at your studying.

-Get up early and go at it for 20 minutes before the kids get up?

-Stay a little late at work, using 5 to 5:30 for Spanish study. Maybe let the traffic die down a little before you head home?

-Lunch hour is study hour. Your headphones on, book in front of you and your sandwich on your lap.

It's your brain that you're working with, and it's your schedule that you're wrestling with, so find a *time* and a *way* that works for you. Make sure you find a way to keep *enjoying* your learning.

I mention this first, because your brain and attitude are the key to your linguistic success.

As excuses come up, overcome them:

"I don't have the time."

Yes you do. We, all of us, have the same 24 hours to work with, and people come up with amazing ways to fill that 24 hours. You can too.

"I'm not getting anywhere." Yes you are. Even though it seems like you forget 2 words for every 1 you learn, you are making progress. It *seems* imperceptible, but each time you study a little more, you are getting a little better. Be patient, like the guy eating the elephant one forkful at a time.

"I need a break." Fine! Give yourself a break. Better to cut yourself some slack and give yourself a rest. Then you can pick it up fresh later. Don't worry if you forget a lot of stuff in the interim. It always comes back faster the second time you learn it.

Here are a few time-management tips for the Spanish (or any language) learner:

- Use the gaps in the day.
  - Waiting for the bus? Pull out some vocabulary cards.
  - Long car commute? Listen to Spanish CD's in the car.
  - Long train commute? Use your laptop to do some Rosetta Stone lessons.
  - Committee meeting on hold for 15 minutes while IT fixes the projector? Out comes your phrase book.
- Always have some learning material on you.
  - In the car. Damn, you got a flat and have to sit and wait while they change it. Do some side-by-side reading during the wait.
  - CD player or iPod always in the backpack or purse. That 10 minute walk at lunchtime to

go get a sandwich, plus time waiting in line at Starbucks, becomes your lesson for the day.

- Teach Yourself Spanish book with you at the airport. Fogged in? Flight delayed? Hey, every waiting room is a Spanish learning center if you're prepared.

- Snap up opportunities as they pop up.
  - That person sitting next to you, also delayed on their flight, just completed a conversation in Spanish on their cell phone. Time to strike up a conversation?
  - Bilingual signs are all over the place. See if you understand the Spanish side of the flight safety card. Now cover up the English side. Now cover up the Spanish side. Quiz yourself.
  - Public announcements are also often given in Spanish, right after the English version. Listen closely, see if you can follow along. If you miss it, don't worry, they make those dumb announcements every 15 minutes!
  - Did you know that most movies you rent come with some language options? So, you just finished watching *Departed*. Watch it again, this time in Spanish. Or try it with Spanish subtitles.
  - As long as we're on movies, there are tons of great movies made in Spanish. Check out *Amores Perros*. Interesting to note – Amores perros means, literally "loves dogs", but it's translated as "Love's a Bitch." We'll touch on the fascinating theme of how titles are translated later.

So come up with a good game plan, and pay a lot of attention to your attitude. The care, feeding, and cultivation of your *attitude* towards learning Spanish is absolutely vital to your success.

Lose that desire, you lose the language.

Keep that desire, you master the language.

Attack on Vocabulary.

2,000 words, man oh man. That's brutal. How the hell am I going to do that?

Maybe you've been out of school for quite a few years, or maybe you're in school and being forced to memorize a lot of other stuff. Either way, "finding room" in your brain for all these words can pose a hell of a problem.

Don't panic. You can do it. Here's a list of ways to "eat this particular elephant."

1. **The common words you're going to use so often, they'll absorb painlessly:**
    -y – and
    -o – or
    -con – with
    -me gusta – I like
    -gracias – thanks
    -por favor – please

2. **A huge number of words are near identical, just pronounced "Spanish-ly":**
    -democracía – democracy
    -presidente – president
    -carro – car
    -weekend – weekend (there is a more Spanish way of saying it, but a lot of them say "weekend" just like we do. An example of "Spanglish.")

    There's nothing wrong with "grabbing the low-hanging fruit", that is, incorporating the words that are really close to English. A ton of verbs fall into this category.
    -Comunicar – to communicate

-Dispensar – to give out (dispense!)
-Identificar – to identify
-Idear – to think up
-Navegar – to navigate (yes, also used to "navigate the web")
-Usar – to use

Hey, they're easy, they're just like English, and there's nothing wrong with "relying on the easy ones."

3. **As your vocabulary increases, more and more you'll be able to "fill in the missing word" by simple reasoning, as mentioned two chapters ago.**

4. **Make your own vocabulary cards with 3 x 5 cards. Write down the things you would say every day, and carry them with you until you have them down.**

   -"Quisiera un billete para el centro." (I'd like a ticket to downtown.) When you buy that ticket on your way to work, say it to yourself. If you start this on Monday, by Thursday you won't need that 3 x 5 card anymore, it'll be in your head.

   -"Abre la boca y di 'Aah'." (Open your mouth and say 'Aah'). Say it to the next Spanish speaking patient that comes into your clinic.

   -"Para completar este puente, necesitamos la aprobacion del comite entero." (To complete this bridge, we need the approval of the entire committee.) If this is a phrase likely to come up at the next town council meeting, practice it ahead of time and "say it" (under your breath, into your cell phone, say it in your imagination) when this issue comes up at the next meeting.

   The idea here is to start incorporating your daily

activities into your vocabulary building. If you're big into horses, then start building your vocabulary around all things pertaining to "caballos" (horses). If you're a butcher, baker, candlestick maker, then build vocabularies first around butcher terms, baker terms, and candlestick terms. These are the terms you use and encounter every day, and learning them will seem more natural.

5. **A lot of people (me included) cannot get anything into their head but that it has to "go up their arm" first. That is, to *learn*, they have to *write it down* first.** Go to Staples, pick up a stack of yellow legal pads, a bunch of pens, and start writing. Write down some phrases and words you need to know on a legal pad. Now, carry that legal pad around with you and sneak a peak at it 10 times a day. Cover up the English, then cover up the Spanish, then go back and forth , back and forth.

Try writing a paragraph out of one of your Spanish books. Copy a poem, and write the English on the other side of the page. Usually, if you write something 3 times, it's going to stay in your head. To reinforce the list, read it into your handy Dictaphone and listen to it while doing the wash or picking up around the house.

It is not easy.

But it can be done. Now, a few tips on "stretching the vocabulary you have."

- When you're talking with Spanish speakers, try, as long as possible, to avoid "bailing out" and going into English.

- When stuck try to find a way "around" the words you don't know until you find a way to say it with the words you DO know.

- A simple trick here is, use the word "not" judiciously. The sample sentences will illustrate.

Sample sentences:
It's hot out and you want to say, "It's hot out." Trouble is, you forgot how to say "hot." So, say, "It's not cold out."

"No hace frío." (It's not cold out.).

Two unexpected bonuses result from this little act of circumnavigation. First, the Spanish speaker thinks you're funny. Here it is 110 degrees in the shade, and you're saying "It's not cold out." Well no kidding! Second, the Spanish speaker will most likely pick up on this and fill in the word you wanted to say.

"Si que no hace frio. Hace mucho calor." (It sure isn't cold today. It's very hot.)

Aha! That's the word you were looking for, "calor."

You're about to introduce your wife to a friend from El Salvador.
"Esta es mi…" (This is my…[damn, what's the word for wife?]) Somehow, you remember the verb form for "getting married", so you say, "Me casé con esta jovencita linda." (I married this young lovely.)
OK, the idea was conveyed, even if a little clunkily. But you fought off the "easy way"; you averted a collapse into English. Hey, you're trying to speak Spanish, so speak Spanish. There's always more than one way to skin the linguistic cat!

You're trying to explain that you're an anesthesiologist.
Anesthesiologist has not yet made its way into your

vocabulary.

"Trabajo en el hospital. (I work in the hospital.) Soy el médico que le hace dormir durante la operación." (I'm the doctor who makes you go to sleep during the operation.)

Once again, the listeners will usually fill in your gaps at this point.

"A, ¿Usted será anestesiologista entonces?" (Oh, so you're an anesthesiologist, are you?)

Aha! You heard it.

"Sí, soy anestesiologista." (Yes, I'm an anesthesiologist.)

So, by working with "what you have" and edging around the weak spots and gaps, you are doing two things:

- You're "staying in the language'. Sticking with Spanish, as long as humanly possible.

- You're picking up vocabulary as you go, as the Spanish speakers fill in for you.

Little by little, that elephant is getting gobbled up.

Any way a Christmas tree can aid our digestion?

Chapter 6

A Christmas Tree

Where have we gotten so far with our assault on learning Spanish by ourselves?

- We shed fear. Learning a language is something to jump into. Fight your way into the heart of Spanish. Forget the mistakes, keep talking!
- We put together some self-learning tips to get you "up and running faster."
  - Do some side-by-side reading.
  - Stick with the most common verb forms and tenses.
  - Record yourself and listen to your self.
  - Get a bunch of different learning programs, and slalom between them.
  - Keep your social antennae up for chances to talk Spanish whenever and wherever you can.

Later, we dug a little deeper into vocabulary and grammar, but still, sticking with the things that give you the best use of your time.

- Common words happen commonly, so build your vocabulary on the common words.
- Use words you can use every day, things that pertain to home or work life.
- Don't shy away from grammar, but stick to those grammar elements that give you the most mileage when it comes to speaking to people.

- Use the present, the two pasts, and fake the future by using the word "ir" (going to) just like we do.
- Know, but don't sweat mistakes, when using the sometimes tough to remember pronouns.
- Do your best to make adjectives and nouns agree, but, again, don't kill yourself if you goof it up every now and again.

Time for a new exercise to stretch your mind, your vocabulary, and your grammar understanding. It takes some high tech equipment.

1. A pen.
2. A notepad.
3. Whichever Spanish book you're working on now.

The Christmas Tree Exercise:

This.
This is how.
This is how it goes.
To learn better, this is how it goes, you see,
If you really have decided to learn better, this is how it goes, you see, you make a Christmas tree.
Ta da!

To expand your ability to express yourself in Spanish, start small with any word you know. Then try to tack words in front or in back of it, making the sentence more and more complicated. Which words should you use? Any? Make up any crazy story you want to, the idea is to use new vocabulary words and to flex your grammatical muscle. If stuck, look something up, or else make your best guess. Usually by the time you're writing all the way across the page, you've exhausted most possibilities.

Then build another Christmas tree.

Here are some examples:

Sí. (Yes.)

¿Sí o no? (Yes or no?)

Quiero saber, ¿sí o no? (I want to know, yes or no?)

Te amo y quiero casarme contigo. Quiero saber, ¿sí o no? (I love you and want to marry you. I want to know, yes or no?)

You start out with the word sí (yes). How hard is that?

Then you make the old, "sí o no" question. (Yes or no.) Still pretty simple.

Now it's time to add a verb, let's use "querer" (to want). *To want* is a verb you'll use a million times in conversation, so it's a good verb to practice. So, we want the present tense, how does that go?

Quiero

Quieres

Quiere

Queremos

Quiere

Quieren

This verb is a little irregular, what with "ie" in some forms, and "e" in others. Quick look in the *201 Spanish Verbs* book to get those forms.

What about the verb following "querer"? Turns out that's in the infinitive, the "to" form, just as it is in English.

I want *to go*, she wants *to leave*, we want *to get* rich.

So, "Quiero saber." is how you say, *I want to know.* Tack that on the earlier phrase, and now our Christmas tree is up to:

Sí. (Yes.)

¿Sí o no? (Yes or no?)

Quiero saber, ¿sí o no? (I want to know, yes or no?)

Where do we go from here? Let's go wild and turn this into a love story. Oh, the drama! We'll profess our love "te amo." That's a good review of those pesky pronouns. Remember, the pronoun comes first, so you're really saying "I you love.." And we can use "querer" again, because we've already reviewed its forms. How do we say "marry"? Pick up the handy dictionary (always have one nearby, you can get a paperback one for a few bucks) and look it up.

What's this? The form is "casarse con" What's this "se" stuck on the end of casar? Hmm, dictionary says it's a reflexive verb. What the hell is that? Pick up your *Teach Yourself Spanish* book and look up reflexive verbs.

Spanish has more reflexive verbs than English. The idea is, the verb "reflects" back onto the person doing the action. In English, we have a few:

-I shave myself (versus, say, a barber shaving someone else)

-I bathe myself (versus, say, a mother bathing a baby)

So in Spanish, when you get married, you actually "marry myself with you," or "casarse con."

But it would make sense, wouldn't it, when you say "with you", to say, "con te", wouldn't it? Where did "contigo" come from?

Turns out, Spanish has a few special forms for "with you (familiar)" and "with me." They are "contigo" and "conmigo." No big deal. It's mentioned in the *Teach Yourself Spanish* book, so it's just one of those things you learn along the way.

Here is the complete Christmas tree, now without the English alongside it:

Sí.

¿Sí o no?

Quiero saber, ¿sí o no?

Te amo y quiero casarme contigo. Quiero saber, ¿sí o no?

A little four line "instant story" that still packs quite a "learning punch:

- Verb review.

- Vocabulary "augmentation."
- Pronoun review.
- Special forms you might not have seen before (contigo, reflexive verbs).

What's so special about the Christmas tree? Why does this help you learn?

YOU made the story up. There's a little emotional tag on this thing, because you created it. YOU had to invent this mini love-encounter, so the story, however trite, has a teeny resonance in your head. Plus, you had to dig for the words in your dictionary and your verb book and your *Teach Yourself* book.

That emotional tag, added to the little digging, makes the Christmas tree lesson memorable. And you'll remember the attached lessons as well.

- Verb review.
- Vocabulary "augmentation."
- Pronoun review.
- Special forms you might not have seen before (contigo, reflexive verbs).

You *own* those four lessons now.

Let's do another couple Christmas trees to nail this down. Then you take over and see how far you can get with them yourself. If you're really pushing it, show your Christmas trees to a Spanish speaking friend and see if they get a kick out of them. While they're chuckling, they'll make a few corrections here and there. And that will help too!

Billete (ticket)
Este billete (this ticket)
Este billete no es mío. (This ticket isn't mine.)
¡Ay, Dios mío! Este billete no es mío. (Oh my God! This

ticket is not mine.)

¡Ay, Dios mío! Este billete no es mío. ¡Es un original del Titanico! (Oh my God! This ticket isn't mine. It's an original from the Titanic!)

¡Ay, Dios mío! Este billete no es mío. ¡Es un original del Titanico! ¡Debe valer una fortuna! (Oh my God! This ticket isn't mine. It's an original from the Titanic! It must be worth a fortune!)

Let's go a little crazy with the next one. We're trying to increase our vocabulary and grammar, not necessarily write something that makes sense! So here goes.

Voy (I'm going)

Voy a comer. (I'm going to eat.)

Sí que voy a comer. (For sure I'm going to eat.)

Sí que voy a comer un elefante entero. (For sure I'm going to eat an entire elephant.)

Sí que voy a comer un elefante entero para el almuerzo. (For sure I'm going to eat an entire elephant for breakfast.)

Now let's take away the English so we get that Christmas tree look.

Voy.

Voy a comer.

Sí que voy a comer.

Sí que voy a comer un elefante entero.

Sí que voy a comer un elefanter entero para el almuerzo.

After you've done a few of these, you'll start identifying the gaps in your knowledge. Here's a good way to measure your progress. Do a few Christmas trees. Go back to your *Spanish in Three Months*, do a few more lessons. Then go back and see how much more oomph you can put into those trees.

You'll go from:

Gusta.

Me gusta mucho.

Cerveza fria me gusta mucho.

En el invierno, cerveza fria me gusta mucho.

(In the summer, I like cold beer a lot.)

To this:

Ojalá.

Ojalá pudiera enumerar.

Ojalá pudiera enumerar a los misticos.

Ojalá pudiera enumerar a los místicos que me guien a la tierra de sabeduría.

(Oh how I wish that I were able to enumerate the mystics who could guide me to the land of knowledge.)

Just the kind of sentence you're likely to use on your first trip to Mazatlán!

So far we seem to be doing great. But what happens the first time we blow it? How do we handle our first big stumble in Spanish? How do we keep on track?

Chapter 7

Keeping it Together After Your First Stumble

Pete Sampras didn't lose too often when he had a tennis racquet in his hand. But even he occasionally tightened up, felt the pressure, dropped a second serve in the net, and missed the "gimme." His approach to these minor failings was characteristic Sampras. "Choking is part of the game," he said in one interview. "It's always there. You have to know that. We are all subject to it." (Not his exact words, but something to that effect.)

What does that have to do with learning a language, and, since we're focused on learning Spanish, what does that have to do with learning Spanish?

Early on, you're going to "choke", you're going to head out into the treacherous waters of this new language, and it's going to desert you and you'll fall flat on your face, convinced that you forgot everything you ever learned. This is the crucial First Stumble, and you want to be prepared for it.

Why even dwell on this?

The care and feeding of your *attitude* toward learning Spanish is crucial. This was mentioned earlier but bears repeating. As long as you remain convinced that learning Spanish is a worthy goal, you'll keep at it. You'll make little recordings, you'll write down Christmas tree exercises, you'll listen to Spanish on the Internet. You'll keep at it. And that's all learning a language takes – keeping at it.

The **First Stumble** poses a real threat to your attitude and your "keep-at-it-ness." Here's how it usually goes.

You've been studying for 3 months, or 6 months, and you've amassed a pretty good grasp of the language. Now it's time to "take the car out for a spin." You accept an invitation to a Cinco de Mayo party at a Mexican colleague's house. This will be mini-immersion at its best, with margaritas to boot! Great action.

You ring the doorbell.

"Hola, bienvenido a la fiesta, entra, entra, ¡estás en tu casa!" (Hello, welcome to the party, come on in, and make yourself at home!)

You have trained your ear for months now, but got a little uptight at the prospect of having to "really do it" as you were walking up the driveway, and what you just heard sounded like, "ioaegnfvxkcfhgmvnuarsgjvneusjghvnuaeorslkdghvnoeuarsgv… norgsjdn."

Now it's into the house, the music's blasting, people are laughing and telling jokes, and you're getting introduced.

"Oye, Juan, este es mi amigo especial del trabajo, y habla con fluidez, no lo creerás!" (Listen, John, this is my special friend from work, and he speaks fluently, you won't believe it.)

Again, your powers of listening seem to have just "up and gone", and now you're not able to pick any individual words out from the lightning fast string that just went by. If you could only slow everything down! Or maybe if people magically had subtitles under what they said, then there'd be enough time to digest the words one   at   a   time and you could start catching on.

Then the people look at you.

Your turn to speak.

On the way up the driveway, you could conjugate about 50 verbs perfectly, had about a 500 word vocabulary, had every "meet and greet" phrase down pat, and seemed like a pretty competent beginner Spanish speaker. Now, in contrast, it feels like someone's glued your tongue to the roof of your mouth, and you can't remember how to count to three, how to say hello, or how to even pronounce your own name with a Spanish accent.

At this point, you have hit the Great Divide! You have

stumbled, you have blanked out, and there are two ways to go.

1. **The "This Shouldn't Have Happened" Approach.**
2. **The Pete Sampras Approach.**

Here's the difference:

1. **This Shouldn't Have Happened.**

   All this work, all this time, all those books, all this blood, sweat and tears, and it's ALL FOR NOTHING! To hell with Spanish. I knew way back when I was no good with this language crap, and now I see it's all true. They all talk too fast to ever understand, and I just screw up and get flustered and forget anyway, so that's it! All that time I spent studying was a waste of time and that's it. I'm done!

2. **Pete Sampras Approach.**

   Choking is part of the game, we're all subject to it. You know it's there, and you deal with it. If Pete Sampras loses a point or a game or a match because he didn't play his best, did he hang up his racquet? Did he say, "All this blood, sweat, and tears, and it's all for nothing!"?

   No, when Pete had a bad day or a bad tournament, if he stumbled, he just kept working at it. No surprise, then, to see him hoisting all those Wimbledon trophies over his head.

   You are in the same boat with your Spanish, especially with your first "tournament", your first attempt to go where you there is a lot of Spanish. Your memory may fail you! A lot of work can go "poof" as your vocabulary suddenly slips out the back door and leaves you gaping like a fish out of water. If you know this is coming, you can deal with it. This becomes just part of the learning process, not some catastrophic, Spanish-ending Apocalypse that dooms all attempts at learning the language. Say to yourself, "This is not my day", then shift gears, get what you can out of the day, and come back swinging the next time.

Let's go back to that Cinco de Mayo party and see how to best handle that **First Stumble**.

Ding dong!

You are pumped, really pumped.

"¡Hola! Bien venido. Pásale, pásale. ¡Oye! Mira por aquí, ¡aquí tiene mi amigo especiál del trabajo!" (Hello, welcome, come on in, come on in. Listen up, look over here, my special friend from work is here!")

You have totally blanked.

You hear, but you don't understand.

You try to speak, but the words catch in your throat.

Someone might just as well have stuck a vacuum cleaner to the Spanish section of your brain and sucked out every single cell.

Options:

- Grab a margarita.
- Flee.
- Pass out.
- Explain your predicament to your hostess.

Well, of course we have to encourage you to take the last option, "Explain your predicament to your hostess.", though we may have to come back to that first option.

Explain your predicament to your hostess.

Just the fact that you are making the effort counts a lot to Spanish speakers. (If you decide to branch out in other languages, you will make a pleasant discovery – the same holds for other languages as well. I've said this before but it's an important point, well worth repeating). At this Cinco de Mayo party, your hostess and her friends are going to welcome you with open arms and encourage your Spanish speaking NO MATTER IF YOU'VE FORGOTTEN EVERYTHING. This is an observation from years of language learning in general and Spanish speaking in particular.

That is the enduring beauty of the entire language scene. If ever there were a "no lose" proposition, it is the realm of speaking languages.

If you're trying at all, that counts a lot. If you butcher the language into a pulpy mess, no one thinks the less of you, because you are trying. So guess what, all your work was NOT in vain, even if you forgot it. Because they know that you were trying.

So, back to the party. Let's call the hostess Elena.

"Elena, listen, thanks for inviting me here, but I've got to tell you something. I don't know if it's nerves or what, but I'm just plain blanking on this stuff. I know I was able to say a few things to you at work, but for some reason, it's just not happening."

By now Elena will have an icy cold margarita in your hand, she'll be shaking her head and waving her hand back and forth.

"Don't worry about it, you're welcome here. Bien?" (OK?)

"Bien." (OK), you say back.

What you have done is:

- Cut yourself some slack.
- "Allowed" yourself to stumble.
- Taken the pressure off – you don't have to be a perfect linguist!
- Since the pressure is off, the "stuff" will start to work again.
- Did you notice Elena said "Bien" and you said "Bien" right back?

Which brings us to the margarita option.

How to phrase this delicately…

"Alcohol assisted language acquisition" has a long and storied history, though few language programs address this "dirty little secret" of the linguistic realm. The following is based, of course, on stuff one *hears*, not, heaven forbid, anything I have actually *done*.

The party's rocking, the music is pounding the paint off the walls, and the Coronas are emptying like magic. Spanish has always been a tough language, with a lot of tricky conjugations and all that feminine/masculine/singular/plural business. But damn, after that third (or was it fourth?) frosty brew, this stuff is coming pretty easy! Hey, what happened to my glass?. It's empty, how did that happen?

There's a solution, and it's right over here in the ice chest.

Time passes, and suddenly, miraculously, the language which seemed impossible so many times is now CAKE! Fluency has arrived with bells and whistles. Never mind that many are the confused looks from those you are attempting to communicate with. Maybe they're not fluent listeners, that's the problem!

Now, a miracle occurs. Fluency in many languages. Some, not yet discovered! Ancient Mayan dialects even Mel Gibson doesn't know about. The language of some visiting space aliens from the Orion nebulae. This, and more, and you are Master and Commander of all of them. Viva Corona! Viva the Corona School of Language Learning!

Lesson learned?

Allow yourself your **First Stumble**.

And maybe get some aspirin and orange juice after last night's party.

We've been working on the HOW of learning Spanish up until now. Let's shift gears, go out into the world, and see the WHY of learning Spanish.

WHY

Chapter 8

Spanish, Sangría and a Rusty Nail. Language in the Real World

In less time than you would have imagined, you've become a Spanish linguist. Yes, you have a lot more work to do, but now you have the magic running through your veins. You will make it happen, because you have the *how* of language.

Let's give you the *why*.

Cool things happen when you learn a language. No doubt.

When you have a foreign language in your hip pocket, you never know when it will come in handy, you never know when some amazing thing or miraculous occurrence will jump out of every day life.

You might impress someone. (Nothing particularly wrong about that.)

You might get a laugh. (Nothing particularly wrong about that either.)

You might save someone from death by tetanus!

Read on. We're going to see that cool things happen when you speak a foreign language.

Cool Things Happen When You Speak Spanish.

A backpack and a Eurail pass and a night in Madrid and a pitcher of sangría. Life is good in España.

Sangría – almost identical to its namesake "sangre" (blood). Red is the sangre that courses through the blood of the Spaniard, and red is the sangría that goes down his throat. Fruity iced wine that festive Spaniards are happy to share with their visiting tourist friends.

So some medical students from America are pouring the sangría down with their new Madrileño friends. Hands clapped on backs, glasses raised, now the songs are starting. What song can the Americans sing for us?

Well, none very well. But that's what the sangría's for!

One more pitcher of sangría, and now they're all eager to sing. *Star Spangled Banner*? No. Something more folksy. How about *Clementine*? Ooh, that's a good one.

So *Clementine* it is.

But such a sad story it is. Darlin' Clementine, dying like that. It's not fair, not fair. She should'a, should'a, where's the sangría?

And now the Madrileños are helping the smitten, sobbing American medical student. Clementine has been too much for him, particularly with half his blood volume, half his "sangre", now replaced by sangría.

"No te preocupes sobre Clementina," the Spaniards say. (Don't worry about Clementine.) "Mas sangría para nuestro amante con corazón roto." (More sangría for our lover with the broken heart.)

"Pero, pero", the med student sobs, "habría amado a Clementina. La habría salvado si pudiera!" (But, but, I would have loved Clementine. I would have saved her if I could.)

Alas. All the love and all the devotion in the world, even that fueled by near-lethal doses of sangría, never allow us access to the inner world of folk songs. We can't pry open those doors, jump in, and snatch Clementine from the closing jaws of death. More's the pity.

"No hay remedio," the Spaniards say, "Mas sangría." (There is no option here. More sangría.)

The Clementine-bereft student takes one last bolt of liquid courage.

Then it's into the cool Madrid night and it's homeward bound. Back to the pensione (a bed and breakfasty kind of place).

Madrid at night is couples walking arm-in-arm, girls walking arm-in arm, and guys walking arm-in-arm. Nothing sexual implied, just the way it's done. The Madriders don't seem as uptight about body contact as Americans. Little cars whiz by, much smaller than American makes. Roads here are skinnier, and parking is a nightmare. The Spaniards double-park all the time, or else they hop onto the sidewalk and park there. A sidewalk is not so much for pedestrians, it's an auxiliary parking spot.

More fresh air, exercise from climbing over cars-on-sidewalks, the sangría buzz just begins to dissipate a tiny little bit. Clementine heads back to the old music sheets and folk festivals, where she belongs.

Madrid's pensiones are scattered around the city center, tucked into brick and stone buildings here and there.

"Which one is it?" The med students are still pretty heavily sangría-ized, and the buildings all look alike.

"That's it." They go into a 6 story brown building.

An open caged elevator holds the promise of an easy ride up to the 4th floor. If it works.

"Let's walk."

On opening the door to the pensione, the med students see their pensione hostess, a woman in her 50's, with her hair in a bun, wearing a loose blue dress with matching blue sweater. Only she's hopping on one foot and holding the other one. And there's blood dripping from the non-hopped-on foot.

Blood!

Sangre!

"El pié", the woman says. (My foot). "Choqué con esto." (I stepped on this.) She holds up a board with a rusty nail sticking out of it. Her blood is on that nail.

The med students are still wasting away again in Sangría-ville, but a woman hopping on one foot and bleeding from another jolts them. It's like seeing a cop's flashing lights. You can't instantly *become* sober, but you instantly *try to become* sober.

The med student takes the board, examines the nail with all

the attentiveness of the trying-to-become-sober investigator.

"Chocó con esto?" (You stepped on this.) Trying to ascertain the facts, get the clues. This is CSI Miami before there even was a CSI Miami. Only it's CSI Madrid, with a heavy fog of alcohol hovering over the investigation.

"Si, ay que me duele." (Yes, oh man, does it hurt.)

Through the fog of ancestral medical knowledge, partly obscured by a thick blanket of sangría, an idea starts bubbling up in the collective conscience of the med students.

Nail.

Stepping on a nail.

Medicine.

Something bad about stepping on a nail.

The student who knows Spanish puts his finger on it and shouts out to the others, "Holy shit, she stepped on a nail. She could get… SANGRÍA!"

"What?"

"Don't you mean tetanus?"

"Of course I mean tetanus."

"But you said…"

"Tétano?" the hopping Spanish woman says.

"Si, tétano. Tenemos que llevarle a un hospital para una injeccion contra tétano." (Yes, tetanus. We have to take you to a hospital so you can get an injection against tetanus.)

Years of pre-med education, four years of Medical School, a zillion dollars in student loans, and the med students collectively come up with something that every third grader knows. If you step on a nail, you can get tetanus.

They must act! Now! Decisively! Or the pensione lady will get deadly lockjaw.

"Absolutely, we have to move." The med students try to harness their weaving energy into some purposeful direction.

The med student who speaks Spanish thinks, "Thank God I speak Spanish. It's dandy to speak it at the bar and win a few 'impress the locals' Brownie points. But man, I really need it now."

As the med students discover, Spain has a weird system of night-time care. No 24 hour emergency rooms with brightly lit entrances. Instead, the slowly sobering students find that they have to track down a 24 hour pharmacy, order a tetanus vaccine, and then find a 24 hour walk-in clinic that can give the injection.

All this requires a hundred starts and stops, all done at a hopping pace and with a dish towel over a bleeding foot.

Finally, the sangría-less med students arrive at a clinic where a General Practitioner will give the fateful tetanus vaccine. The med students eye the doctor up and down, wondering if he's sufficiently qualified to administer the shot. They are mother lionesses by now, guarding their wounded cub.

"¿Cuando graduó?" (When did you graduate?) This fellow looks pretty young.

Another student says, "Ask him if he has any resuscitative equipment around, you know, in case she has an allergic reaction or something."

Message delivered. The Madrid doctor shrugs and says, "Vamos a manejar." (We'll manage somehow.)

Jaundiced looks from the lionesses.

Injection given. No allergic reaction. Wound washed, bandage applied. All is well, and *this* Clementine will not be joining the Clementine of song. The pensione hostess is delivered from the jaws of death, more accurately, from the lockjaws of death.

It's 3:40 AM before the med students hit the sack at the pensione.

"Lucky I knew Spanish."

Good things happen when you speak a foreign language.

Ecuador, three years later. On a medical mission with Interplast, a group that provides plastic surgery to third world countries. They specialize in cleft lip, cleft palate, and burn scar repairs.

You don't *have* to speak the natives' language to go on these trips, but all the surgeons, anesthesiologists, and nurses make a point of learning the basics. But it's damned handy to have at least one person on the team who is fluent. Especially for the preoperative visits, you want someone who can ferret out a good medical history to avoid "discovering something" in the operating room and getting in trouble. Plus, at the end of the trip, it's good to have someone who can deliver a nice farewell speech to the host country in their own language.

The trip attracts a Fellini-movie mix of characters from all across America.

One plastic surgeon comes from Cincinnati with a bicyclist's build and a raconteur's bag of stories from earlier Interplast trips. Two years before, he'd been on a trip to Honduras. As his young patient was being placed on the operating room table, he noted a whiteness covering the surface of the patient's left eye. Too young for a cataract, something traumatic must have happened to this eye.

"What happened to his eye here?" the surgeon asks the translator.

"Oh, last year he come in for to take off wart on face," the translator says. "When doctor, he moving hand over face, he accident drop knife and fall in boy's eye. Then eye get all white after that."

"Oh,", the bike-riding plastic surgeon says, no condemnation in his voice, no judgment seeping around the edges. "I hate it when that happens."

From Abilene comes a big bruising plastic surgeon. He'd be at home playing tackle for the Dallas Cowboys. Between cases and at the end of the day he spins yarns in a molasses Texas accent. Most stories center on the two night time activities available in Abilene – drinking beer and getting in knife fights. During most of his fights, the surgeon had his brother (also in the 6'4", 250 pound of solid muscle range) at his side.

"What does your brother do now?" one of the nurses asks

him. "Bouncer at the Mustang Ranch? Cop?"

"Nope," the Texan says. "Not a bouncer, ain't a cop. Went hisself to Wisconsin and got him an art appreciation degree. Now he's a professor of Fine Arts up there.

"Somehow, back there in Texas, swingin' them bottles around and bustin' them over heads in a bar parkin' lot, I just didn't figure him for a Renoir and Monet man."

The chief surgeon hails from North Carolina. Accompanying him on this trip, his wife. On his last trip? His mistress. The surgeon lives with both, along with sundry children from both, in one happy Brady-Bunch-with-a-twist household in the mountains of North Carolina.

How do his neighbors view this chummy set-up? He placates the local gentry with frequent parties, including naked romps in his cedar wood hot tub. So who's to complain?

But the platinum blond (at the ends) jet black (at the roots) plastic surgeon from Seattle takes first prize in this lineup. In her waterfront condo, the woman harbors an illegal immigrant. Horrors! Some Mexican who swam across the Rio Grande and made his way to the Emerald City? Not exactly. Her illegal immigrant hails from Belgium.

Belgium! America threatened by a human tidal wave of immigrants riding bicycles and carrying chocolates. What a nightmare!

"What does this Belgian do?" the Cincinnati surgeon asks his colleague. We're at a local pub, gasping in the thin air of the Andes and salving our pain with the local brew. The Texan is nearby in case a fight breaks out.

"He in school or what?" the North Carolina sort-of-polygamist asks.

The woman shakes her head. "He, uh, takes care of me, if you know what I mean."

We knew.

The surgical team hadn't cornered the market on characters. Heading the anesthesia team is a Taiwan native who moved to New York at age 9, so he had a Brooklyn accent. He was a perpetual motion machine.

College in Fairbanks, Alaska. "The weather there is perfect, no kidding."

Anesthesia training in Chicago, Sri Lanka, and Australia. "Hey, you move around, you see there's more than one way to skin a cat, or, in Australia, more than one way to skin a kangaroo."

Visited Leningrad in the dead of winter. "No tourists. Had the whole Hermitage to myself."

Crossed India by rail just to see the place close up. "OK, so it's dirty. Do you want to spend all your vacations at a Des Moines Holiday Inn?"

Tramp freighter trip to Singapore. "Best sushi in Singapore. Better even than Japan."

Ate chilled monkey brains in Istanbul. "It's awful. Don't try it if offered, just take that on faith from me."

Has a recipe for home-made eyewash. "The Korean riot police use pepper spray at the drop of a hat. Always have a little eyewash on you if you get caught in a riot there."

Oh Brave New World, that has such people in it.

What the hell does this have to do with language?

One thing this whacko contingent had in common, along with their unflappable demeanor ("I hate it when that happens."), their appetites ("He takes care of me."), and their culinary habits ("Don't eat monkey brains."), was this – they all taught themselves enough Spanish to get by.

The Cincinnati surgeon found a way to stretch a minimal vocabulary to maximal effect!

An expert on melanoma (a skin cancer), the Cincinnatian usually gave the local medicos a talk on melanoma.

"I'm not so good at languages," the surgeon says. "So I just keep throwing up slides with pictures of the different kinds of melanoma. The names are written underneath the picture, and the names are the same in English and Spanish."

"After they look at it a while, I say, 'Es típico.' (It's typical)."

Slide – "Es típico."

Next slide – "Es típico."

On through the rest of the talk, finishing on the last slide with a final, "Es típico."

"They love it!" the plastic surgeon says. "An ENTIRE talk and it's all in Spanish. I come across as fluent!"

Mario Pei, one of the greatest linguists of all time, maintains that real fluency in a language requires a vocabulary of 2,000 words. Ha! The Cincinnati guy found a way to be fluent with TWO words. Genius!

The guts of the trip are the operations. And Maria Luisa, a nine year old girl, was the toughest one of all. Her story was a common one among los indios (the indigenous people) of the area.

The anesthesiologist fluent in Spanish served as the preoperative doctor, and got the story of Maria Luisa.

Loja (a city of about 100,000 people, high in the Andes mountains of Ecuador) held the hospital, and the surrounding mountains held most of los indios. No electricity reaches up into the small villages, so houses are lit with lámparas (lamps). As babies do everywhere, los bebés de los indios (the babies of the indios) were forever grabbing things and pulling at them. Maria Luisa, as a baby, had pulled a tablecloth and an oil lamp had fallen on her, burning her face, especially her lower lip, and her chest.

In a developed country, she would have gotten specialty help with her burn. But in the mountains, she got no care at all. If a child dies up there, it's most often attributed to "la voluntad de Dios" (the will of God) As she healed, the different burned areas scarred together. Her lower lip was sealed to her chest, her head kept in a grotesque downward tilt. She was unable to close her mouth, and saliva ran down the front of her shirt.

The mother of Maria Luisa asked us, "¿Puede ayudarle?" (Can you help her?) She gave a look you couldn't forget. Maria Luisa looked up (she always had to look up) and asked the same question "con los ojos." (With her eyes.) She couldn't close her mouth well enough to say anything "con la boca." (With her mouth.)

"Sí, se puede." (Yes, it can be done.)

The Seattle surgeon with the Belgian stallion-in-waiting got the nod for the operation.

Anesthetizing her was tough, the shape of her face making it hard to place the endotracheal tube (the breathing tube that goes into the windpipe). Once she was under, the surgeon took over.

"Tijeras, tijeras," she kept asking. (Scissors, scissors.) All the scrub nurses came from Loja so asking for instruments was all done in Spanish. The Loja hospital had the simplest of instruments, nothing exotic or expensive, so the plastic surgeons had to do most of their work with scissors and ingenuity.

"Tijeras, algo mas…how do you say sharp?" she asks the anesthesiologist.

"Agudas."

"Tijeras mas agudas, por favor." (More sharp scissors, please.)

First she separates the scar tissue connecting the lower lip to the chest, careful not to damage the lip itself. The muscles around the mouth are uniquely designed to let you close your mouth, eat, suck from a straw, speak. Rending the lip apart will undo all that. But the lip is buried in tons of scar, and telling years-old scar from delicate lip tissue is no mean feat.

Hours of dissecting. Once the scar tissue is separated, the surgeon pulls Maria Luisa's head back, taking it out of that permanent "leaning forward" posture. The scar tissue cracks and pops like gristle. People in the room groan.

"Tijeras, tijeras."

The Seattle surgeon does a lot of "Z-plasties." Cutting a Z

shape in the scar, undoing the thick, underlying scar, and sewing things back together in a normal anatomic shape.

Four hours of work, then Maria Luisa is in the recovery room, neck swaddled in bandages. Her lips are now on her face.

"Bien hecho," (Well done,) the nurse tells the surgeon.

The surgeon turns to the anesthesiologist. "What did she say?"

"She said you know what you're doing, doc."

The next morning, the anesthesiologist stops by to see Maria Luisa. She is sitting up in bed. In her hands she holds a can of 7-Up, a straw sticking out the top. She is taking a sip.

Maria Luisa's lips could fit around a straw for the first time since the burn.

She takes her lips off the straw and smiles.

"Gracias, doctor."

Now she could speak, clear as a bell.

Things happen when you speak a language.

Chapter 9

How About Making the Leap to Multi-Linguist?

My Dad spoke a boatload of languages. I speak fluent Spanish, French, German, Italian, and Portuguese. I can hold my own at a conversational level in Russian, Mandarin, Japanese, Dutch, Swedish, and Polish. In a limited sense, I can make myself understood in Greek, Hebrew, Arabic, Serbo-Croatian and probably something else, I forget myself.

How did my father learn all those languages, and how did I?

Read on. If *we* did it, so can *you*. Keep this in mind always, learning a language, or a bunch of languages, is not a matter of brilliance. It is a matter of persistence and doggedness.

If you work at them, you'll get them.

What, we're done with Spanish already? We've just stuck our baby toe into it! Don't tell me we're going to spread our wings so soon!

Sooner or later, you have to wrestle this Brahma bull to the ground for yourself. At what point do you "take a detour" and start learning other languages, versus "staying put" and working on, say, Spanish?

1. **You only have so much time in the day.**
2. **You only have so much gray matter between your ears.**
3. **Do you keep pouring your energy into Spanish until you're fluent/a lot better/a little better?**
4. **Do you go the multi-lingual route early on, using Spanish to help you learn another language?**
5. **Do you wait? How long do you wait?**
6. **Will the "time away from Spanish" hurt your Spanish?**

7. Will you start mixing up the "new" languages?

Good questions all! Only one way to answer these questions, with another story!

On a train in Switzerland.

A Junior Year Abroad woman from Iowa, spending her year in Paris, is taking advantage of her Eurail pass to zip around and see the sights. Across from her, a fellow traveler is asking the very questions listed above.

She's learning French, is she trying to learn some other languages, too?

"No. I don't want to mix up the French I learned!" she says. She is sitting in a 6 person compartment, the train winding through the mountains of Switzerland, on its way to Italy.

"Maybe you could learn a little Italian, you know, just for the trip. They're pretty close, Italian and French."

The Swiss have carved an amazing number of tunnels through the Alps. Into a tunnel, the outside turns pitch black, a few seconds later, bright sunshine and another postcard-perfect Swiss mountain valley pops into view. Steep roofed chalets, goats on slanting meadows. Then dark, then a different valley, then dark again.

"Well, I know 'ciao' and 'grazie,' but, really, I'll mix up my French if I really learn Italian," the Iowan says.

Fair enough, there's no law that says you have to learn more than one foreign language. Bravo to her for learning French!

Tunnel, valley, dark, bright.

The compartment door opens and in walks a guy right out of GQ magazine.

"Posso sentare qui?" (May I sit here?) he asks in Italian.

"Come vorebbe", (Sure), the fellow traveler says. In this traveler's lap is *Teach Yourself Italian*.

The Iowa woman is not entirely displeased that this Italian man has chosen this compartment, from all the other compartments, to sit in. Any casual observer would note that her eyes were serving as conduits to pour her heart, soul, and other parts unmentioned into the Italian guy's eyes. If looks were deeds, this would be the honeymoon suite and the fellow traveler would be getting ushered out, thank you.

"Ciao", the Iowan says. "Grazie."

She has fired her entire supply of cannonballs, as far as the Italian language is concerned.

The Italian smiles at her. Pearly whites, straight as a ruler. Between them, the air is hot enough to smelt iron.

Dark, bright, dark, bright. Through the tunnels.

Within three tunnels, Our Lady of the French Only has the *Teach Yourself Italian* book in her lap, the Italian guy by her side, her first Italian lesson going, and the fellow traveler looking for another compartment.

The woman from Iowa answers the question, "When do you move on to another language?"

You move on when the opportunity presents itself! When you meet a person who speaks something you don't, and you want to speak with that person, learn that language! Go for it. Let's go over the problems with jumping into another language before you "have the first one down."

1. You only have so much time in the day.

Tough. To do amazing things (like learn a bunch of languages), you have to make amazing use of your time. Try this for starters – go to bed early, stop watching so much stupid television. And quit trolling on You Tube for indecent shots of movie stars getting out of cars in manner most inelegant. There's a lot of time in a day if you don't waste your time.

2. You only have so much gray matter between your ears.

Don't believe it. No matter how much language stuff you've learned, you can keep squishing more into your thick skull if you keep at it. There is no "Full" sign on anybody's brain, ever.

3. Do you keep pouring your energy into Spanish until you're fluent/a lot better/a little better?

Keep at everything. Set aside a little time each week to review your Spanish, even as you're moving on to Italian or French or whatever. The good thing about having a few languages "under construction", is that you have more chances to practice. You see the neighbor from Argentina – talk Spanish to them. At work you bump into someone from Quebec – practice your French with them. Lo and behold, a visitor from Rome – practice your Italian with him. As you get more languages "on board", the whole world turns into "someone you can practice with."

4. Do you go the multi-lingual route early on, using Spanish to help you learn another language?

Amen you use Spanish to help you with another language.

Yo voy (I go) becomes *Je vais* in French, *io vado* in Italian, *eu vou* in Portuguese.

Those are pretty similar looking, and they're pretty close sounding too. This has been mentioned earlier but bears repeating. To learn the "first" language in a group takes a lot of effort. To learn the second, third, and fourth in a group takes way less effort.

5. Do you wait? How long do you wait?

Depends on you. The good news is, taking on a new language is always a "no lose" proposition. Say you decide to learn French, and you only learn a few phrases, then stall out there. Hey, no one *expects* you to know any French, so just knowing those few phrases puts you "ahead of the game." If you learn a little French, then get swamped by life and have to lay off for a year or two, no problem. If you decide to come back to it, it'll be easier to learn it anew. You'll be surprised how much is "left over" even after a long layoff.

6. Will the "time away from Spanish" hurt your Spanish?

It could. But if you've already set up good habits:
-listening to Spanish radio stations
-watching some Spanish TV (language TV is OK!)
-talking every time you meet a Spanish speaker
then you will be OK. You'll find yourself "shoring up the Spanish" even as you're "putting new additions" on your linguistic house.

7. Will you start mixing up the "new" languages?

Yes. But that mistake is no more fatal than any other mistake you make. Speaking means slipping up! You're sticking your neck out there, and a bunch of times, you'll blow it. You'll get mixed up. So what? Especially if you're in the Romance language group, the similarities are so close that they'll still understand you. No fear! Like the T-shirts say.

What tools do I use when I start adding on other languages?

For that answer, we go to Tiger Woods.

Tiger Woods has, according to those who know golf, one swing. Whether he's driving, chipping, or putting, he does the same thing every time. He lines up the same, watches the ball the same, follows through the same (obviously, there's a little difference in energy expenditure between a 300 yard drive and a 3 inch putt). He practices that swing and executes that swing over and over and over again.

He's on track to be the first billionaire sports figure and the greatest golfer in history.

His method, then, begs emulation.

Use the same techniques to learn other languages that you used to learn Spanish. Let's review them.

- Abandon fear. Jump into the language with both feet. Don't sweat the mistakes.

- Set yourself up to learn 2 languages
  - Receiving
  - Sending

- Immerse yourself in the language right away. As you go farther and farther afield, some languages get a little harder to find. Use the Internet! You can pick up every language on the planet with a little surfing.

- Get that Dictaphone, that *Pimsleur* lesson, that *Teach Yourself* book. Jump in and start doing lessons on your own. Learn how to pronounce right away so your self-recordings will be worthwhile lessons. Record yourself and listen to yourself. The more "tools" you use (listening, reading, writing, speaking), the more will sink in.

- Find a native to practice with. It's a global village out there. There's people *from* everywhere *living* everywhere. Keep your antennae up. Know who's from where.

- Start right in with the dual-language work. Again, Internet to the rescue. Get an easy book in the language you want to learn (kid's book, Agatha Christie mystery) and get the English translation. Lay them side-by-side and go for the gusto.

- Slalom from phrase book to grammar lessons (Don't limit yourself like Polly the Parrot!) to CD to DVD. Get a movie in that language and watch it with subtitles, then cover up the subtitles and watch it again.

- Remember that the price is always right at the public library and the librarian will help steer you in the right direction.

- Jump into the verbs, learning the "I" and "you" forms first, and sticking with the present and one past form. Build up the more complicated tenses later.

- Keep at it. It's persistence, not brilliance, which gets you speaking.

Does this sound familiar? Of course it does. It's all the same things you did to learn Spanish. You use the same technique all the time, just like Tiger Woods uses the same stroke all the time.

Too bad there aren't any billionaire linguists.

We've been working pretty hard. Time for a little break.

We saw before how "Cool Things Happen When you Speak Spanish." What happens when we branch out and learn a few more languages, what other adventures await us?

Chapter 10

The Cookie that Ended the Cold War: Russian

Washington DC, the Smithsonian Air and Space Museum.

The model of the starship Enterprise hangs overhead. NCC-1701 printed on the top. To think, it all happened there, right in the guts of that starship. Captain James T. Kirk and the whole Star Trek gang, weaving through three years of intergalactic, warp-speed mayhem, and, of course, all the loving that Kirk could handle from a slew of filmily clad humanoids.

Big Bang indeed.

And by now (1984), the show had been through 17 years of reruns. "The City on the Edge of Forever", that was a good one, maybe the best. "The Trouble with Tribbles." Why *did* they take that show off the air?

Each show a little morality play. Good guys in white hats, bad guys in black. And Star Trek didn't just push the space/time envelope. They pushed the public's envelope too. Kirk, a white man, kissing Uhura, a black woman. That didn't play well in Dixie! And the censors nearly lost it too. Can black/white kissing go on in prime time America? It was, after all, only 100 years since the Civil War. We can't rush into these things, pell-mell.

Star Trek laid out the whole world, too. The Federation stood for the USA and the "good guys" of NATO. The rough-speaking, ever-menacing Klingons stood for the USSR and the ever-threatening Warsaw Pact. The Federation and the Klingons squared off and stood at drawn daggers across an Iron Curtain, stretched taut across the entire universe. And Ronald Reagan's USA and Michael Tikhonov's USSR stood at drawn ICBM's across a barbed-wire, minefield, and machine-gun covered Iron Curtain that ran "from Stettin in the Baltic to Trieste in the Adriatic."

Winston Churchill had said that in 1946. At the time of the Star Trek series, 1969, the Berlin Wall was 8 years old; it appeared to be a permanent part of the world landscape. Now, in a 1984 world, the Wall seemed ready to stand for a million years, the battle lines and attitudes between East and West as hardened as the concrete wall itself.

Reagan was waving his Star Wars strategic defense initiative at that wall now. Star *Wars*, what was he thinking? He should call it the Star *Trek* strategic defense initiative. *Star Trek* beat *Star Wars* all hollow. *Star Trek* was class, not just computer generated trickery.

Just look at the Enterprise hanging there.

That is cool.

The Enterprise could bring that Berlin Wall down, with one little photon torpedo.

Stepping back, it's easy to look over the entire model. Four feet long, hanging on strings, at a tilt, you can see the lettering on top, the living quarters, the bridge, everything. One more step back.

Strange sounds start rumbling up from a knot of people a few feet back. Harsh sounds, at first unintelligible. Klingon?

No.

Russian.

They are speaking Russian, the language on the *other* side of the Iron Curtain. A group of about 30 people are clustered around, the ones in the center speaking Russian and a bunch of people around them seeming to herd them around.

What are a bunch of *Russians* doing in the Air and Space Museum?

What are a bunch of *Russians* doing this close to the Enterprise?

The group moves on and a tour guide keeps talking to them. He points at overhanging historic planes and rockets and gives them the schpiel in Russian.

"Who are they?" I ask to no one in particular.

Some guy next to me says, "Those Russian guys? They're the ones from the shipwreck.?

"What shipwreck?"

The guy looks at me and raises an eyebrow, "Where have you been all week? Mars?"

Not Mars, exactly, but traveling around the country, interviewing for anesthesia residencies. Hadn't watched much TV, hadn't listened to much radio, hadn't read any newspapers. Might as well have been on Mars.

"I've been a little out of touch, tell me about this shipwreck."

A Soviet freighter had foundered off the coast of North Carolina the week before. The US Coast Guard came to the rescue and saved all the crewmen. Reagan was beside himself with "we showed them" Cold Warriorsmanship.

"We rescued the bastards and now we're going to kill them with kindness!"

A million megatons of nuclear destruction ready to rain down from them onto us, and the same amount of death ready to rain down from us onto them. But for now, we were going to play the gracious host, and take the now-dried-off sailors on a tour of DC's museums.

The media went nuts.

The CIA went nuts (wouldn't it be great if some of them defected!).

The KGB from the Soviet embassy went nuts (no way any of them are going to defect!).

So this tour group looked like a cross-section of a tree, with concentric rings. At the center, the happy-to-be-rescued crewmen of the freighter. Clustered around them in the first ring, KGB goons making damned sure no one made a break for it. ("Hey, Nikolai, thinking of moving to New York? Remember, we know where your family lives. Life can be very hard for your 5 year old daughter living in Siberia without her father.") Around this protective ring is the "temptation ring", the American "tour guides" (who all miraculously speak Russian!) who are more than ready to assist any dash for political asylum.

In the center of the Air and Space Museum, the concentric rings look like this:

-a dozen or so young men and one older man. They are wearing sailor-ish uniforms (Coast Guard hand-me-downs?).

-around them, another dozen men, all big and imposing, wearing grubby coats and sour looks on their faces. Their fashion sense is 20 years out of date, looking like spies in a *Get Smart* TV episode.

-flitting around in the outermost orbit are a bunch of sharp-dressed men, younger than their Russian counterparts.

Everyone might as well be wearing nametags.

HELLO, MY NAME IS WARREN, I WORK FOR THE CIA, MAY I HELP YOU?

Would it not be the coolest thing in the world to walk up to these Soviet sailors, these members of the "Evil Empire", these inhabitants of the Klingon side of the Iron Curtain?

But to do that, to peek over the Iron Curtain, to slip into the Evil Empire and talk with the Klingons, would require a knowledge of Russian.

No problem.

So the Russian-speaking med student (me) does just that.

Past the sharp-dressed CIA tour guides. They look at each other. Who is this? He's not one of ours.

Past the scruffy KGB goons. They look at each other. Kto eta? On nyet u nas. (Who is this? He's not one of ours.)

Into the crowd of Russian sailors and the conversation starts up.

"Kak dyela? Ya uslishal chto vi nashi gosti. Vam nravitsya eta museya?" (How's it going? I heard you're our guests. Do you like the museum?)

The grammar is not perfect, the pronunciation even less so.

The vocabulary is limited.

But it's understandable. The Russians start talking to the American.

The KGB guys do NOT like this. Nyet f poryadek. (Not on the schedule.)

The CIA guys do NOT like this. Not on the schedule. Who is this schmuck coming out of the crowd and walking up to these VIP's?

After a little chit chat, the sailors introduce the visitor to the ship's doctor, the older member of the crew. Since the American is just finishing medical school, there's a little doc-to-doc palaver. A couple of old Medicine Men swapping tales of nostrums, unguents, and physic. In a minute, they're thick as thieves.

After a few minutes, the medical student has to take his leave. He's running out of the ability to understand the Russians as they talk faster and faster. But he doesn't *have* to understand everything. He's understood *something*. And he's made a *connection*.

He has spoken to the Klingons in their own tongue. He's seen the Evil Empire for himself. He's spun the magic.

But there's one thing yet.

"Moy drook", (my friend) "U menya odeen vyesch dlya tebya" (I have one thing for you). The student has forgotten the word for "gift" and says "one thing" instead. You don't have to speak perfectly to be understood.

He reaches inside his jacket, a faded green Army issue you might see on a street person.

Everyone's eyes bulge.

The KGB guys (who may well be packing heat) see this unknown guy "going for something" in his jacket.

The CIA guys (who for *sure* are packing heat) see this unknown guy "going for something."

All this in 2nd Amendment besotted, gun-drunk America.

Red alert, all around.

Out of the Army jacket comes a bag of chocolate chip

cookies, home-baked that morning, still warm enough to have put a little moisture (steam gone to water) on the inside of the plastic bag.

"Dlya nashey druzhbay, myezhdoo Amerikay ee Say Say Say Er." (To our friendship, between America and the USSR.)

The doctor takes the cookies from the med student.

Five years later, the Berlin Wall crumbles.

Cool things happen when you speak a foreign language.

Chapter 11

History on the Hoof: French

Sounds echo all over the cavernous Gare de l'Est (East Station) in Paris. Announcements of train arrivals and departures, all in French, bounce off the huge straight walls and the curved roof. The place generates the acoustic garble of a football stadium halftime show. Even a professor in the **Académie française** would have a hard time understanding what was said.

But no one has to understand any announcements – the signs above the platforms roll over every few minutes. Fip fip fip fip fip! The train to Munich is on platform 5, to Amsterdam on platform 8. Fip fip fip fip fip! New trains, new platforms.

With Eurail pass in hand, the adventuresome traveler can go anywhere he wants. The year is pre-Berlin Wall collapse (though that has been set in motion by an exchange of cookies at Washington DC's Air and Space Museum), so the Eurail pass says, "Go anywhere you want, as long as it's *this* side of the Iron Curtain." A meager store of traveler's checks says "Go wherever you want, as long as you stay out of expensive restaurants and sleep in crummy youth hostels."

The stay in France has gone well, much better than expectations. The usual fluff had been thrown around:

- You'll hate France, they're all conceited.
- If you speak French, they'll pretend not to understand you.
- They'll laugh at your pronunciation.
- Don't even try to speak French over there.

Just hadn't happened.

Go in with the expectation, "The French hold their language in high esteem, more so than we do." OK. Fine. It's their country. It's their thing. No reason to get your underwear all tied up in a knot over it.

It's a tough language (all languages are, in their own way, tough), but it's doable with the usual method – work at it.

Pronunciation is particularly thorny, with a lot of silent letters at the end of words, lots of exceptions to rules, and a kind of gargly "r" that takes some effort. But it's a Romance language, ultimately linked via Latin to many European languages (Spanish, Italian, Portuguese) and indirectly linked to English. (By the way, you don't have to learn Latin first, you're better off learning Spanish first and using that as a jump off to the other Romance languages.)

Village, in French, *village*, just pronounced differently.

Civilization, in French, *civilization*, just pronounced differently.

Not impossible. Or, in French, *impossible* (just pronounced differently).

Right at the border of France, the work on French starts to pay off.

"Vous etes americain?" the border guard asks. (Are you American?)

"Oui, ou dois je dire oc?" (Yes [in the Parisian way of pronouncing], or should I say yes? [pronounced in the French accent of the Languedoc region, where the train was crossing the border])

The guard smiles at this "inside the realm of the French language" joke. This tourist knows a little bit about France's most treasured heritage, its native tongue!

And that's the way to play it in France. OK, the French dig their language, so go with the linguistic flow on this. When in Rome, do as the Romans. When in France, do as the French-language-loving French.

A bike trip to Normandy pays off in spades, both from a

history and a language point of view. The landing beaches of D-Day, 1944. Omaha Beach. History up close and personal, as you walk the very sand that those soldiers had to cross so long ago. Only now there's no gunfire or smoke, just a few other tourists walking around, taking it all in.

Is there anyone around now who was there then? Anyone who remembers the war years? Lot of time has passed.

At a bed and breakfast in Normandy, the knowledge of French again pays off.

"Mais, vous parlez français si bien. Est-ce que tu voudrais une goutte de cidre?" A thirty-ish innkeeper says. (But you [in the formal, "vous", sense] speak French so well. Would you [now shifted to the more informal "tu" form] like a drop of cider?) From "vous" to "tu" in two sentences. This is a linguistic promotion!

Normandy cider (they grow a lot of apples there) can be pretty strong stuff. That "goutte" turned into quite a few "gouttes" and quite the hangover the next day.

Then it's back to Paris, take in the sites, ride the boat down the Seine, see the city of lights at night, eat a lot of crêpes in the Montparnesse area. And always the knowledge of French helping. In the restaurants, the coffee shops, hanging out by Notre Dame. Speaking French, not perfectly, not fluently, but getting understood, is the key to the whole experience. Seems the French are not the monsters of legend. They are quite nice once you get to know them. Surprise, surprise.

But now it's time to leave, so it's off to the Gare de l'Est, the point of departure for all points east of Paris. East and a little north gets you into Belgium and then Holland. Straight east and you hit tiny Luxumbourg. Just a hair south and you hit France's sometimes problematic neighbor, Germany.

Back in 1944, this station was packed with a lot of people heading for Germany. Germans heading for Germany. Occupying German soldiers, fast losing their grip on France as Allied troops made their way off the Normandy beaches and pushed the Germans back. And the only train station for points east was this one, the Gare de l'Est.

What must it have been like?

Fip, fip, fip, fip, fip. The letters on the departure board flip over again.

Munich, 18:30, 9.

So the train to Munich (why not go there next?), leaves at 6:30 PM from platform number 9. That leaves about 2 hours to kill before jumping on board. Maybe there's some place nearby where we can wet our whistle. Maybe get another "goutte" or two of that Norman cider before we see how Munich's beer compares.

Across from the station, a small café crooks its finger and offers a perfect place to spend a few hours. Inside, dark, smoky (it seems like everyone in Europe smokes!). One couple sits in the back eating sandwiches and pommes frites (French fries, but don't call them French fries to the French!) Behind the bar, one man holds the fort.

That desire for "history on the hoof" hits. The barkeep looks old enough to have been in Paris during the German occupation. Maybe a little conversation will open up a treasure trove of experience.

"Une verre pour moi, et encore pour vous, monsieur." (A glass for me, and another for you.) "Encore" might not be the right word, but it seems the right idea. The bartender accepts and pours himself a glass, so it must have been right.

Time passes, glasses fill and empty, some bread is broken and shared. Outside, Parisians drive using their horns as a kind of echo-location device.

"Est-ce que vous etiez ici pendant la guerre?" (Were you here during the war?)

"Mais oui," the barkeep says. (Well, yes.)

Jackpot.

The man owned and worked in this very café during the occupation, and was here when the Germans used the Gare de l'Est to get out.

"Quand ils gagnaient, ils etaient insopportables." (When they were winning, they were unsupportable? No wait, don't translate too literally, it must mean "insufferable." That works, "When they were winning, they were insufferable.")

"Pas de pourboires, tu sais?" (They didn't even leave tips. You know what I mean.)

Funny how all the cruelty of war, the fire and destruction, the death, and this is what made a big impression on the bartender. And sitting there, you could understand it. What a damned rotten thing that is to do, not leave a tip. You conquer and occupy a country, and what's more, you don't tip the poor working stiffs under your heel.

For the next hour, he recounts life under the swastika. Never enough food, people arrested, people shot. And always the hope the Allies would come. Always the belief that, one day, Paris would be rid of these pests.

"Ils etaient les maitres de Paris, ils en avaient tous, ils ne craignaient rien." (They were the masters of Paris. They had it all. They feared nothing.)

Forever it seemed like the Germans couldn't lose.

"Nous, puis les Russes. On croyait que c'etait le fin du monde." (Us, then the Russians. You thought it was the end of the world.)

Instead of history from books or old black and white newsreels, this was history come to life. This man had been there. He had seen history, had lived it.

Then news of the invasion. He heard about it from a friend in the Resistance. Germans tried to jam the radio signals, but the broadcasts came. Parisians started to smile. Everyone was skinny (the Germans had taken all the food), but there was hope. Rescue was coming!

The barkeep wondered, would the Germans blow Paris

apart? He walked around, saw the dynamite charges under the Eiffel Tower, under the Pont Neuf. Would they kill everyone before they left? It would be like the Germans to do that.

Rumbles to the west and northwest. Flashes at night. Not the flashes of air raid bombs, these were the more constant drumbeat of artillery.

Girlfriends of the Germans, so cocky in the early years, were looking worried. They'd backed what seemed like the winning horse. But that horse did not seem to be winning anymore.

Then it got hard to sleep, the rumbles were so loud.

"Maintenant ils perdaient, et ils en savaient." (Now they were losing, and they knew it.)

But now it was time to leave. To catch the train to Germany, of all places.

The barkeep walks to the door of the café and points to the Gare de l'Est.

"Ils partaient la, et ils avaient peur." (They left there, and they were scared.)

Cool things happen when you speak a foreign language.

Chapter 12

What Stuff that Dreams are Made of: Italian and Portuguese

Capri rises like a big saddle out of the Mediterranean just off the coast of Naples, Italy. Approachable only by ferry, the island dares you to try to land. The mountains drop straight into the sea. Only one way for boats to approach – via man-made concrete jetties. How anyone got on Capri before those things were built is a mystery. Just after you get off the boat, it's all uphill. Capri the town drapes itself across the mountains' contours, with long, winding alleyways that slither between buildings. No cars can squeeze through these streets, so deliveries are made with special little vehicles that look like golf carts.

It's easy to get lost in Capri.

When you look for Hadrian's Villa (a Roman ruin – somehow Hadrian got himself and a whole construction crew onto Capri), it's easy to take a wrong turn. You might find yourself wandering toward Il Arco Naturale (the Natural Arch – a spectacular natural formation just a little ways out in the water).

And there you stand, guidebook in hand, scratching your head, looking at a guidebook.

There stands a young Italian woman, sweeping her porch. A wire fence between alleyway and porch serves as chaperone and guardian of propriety between the lost tourist and the young sweeper.

"Scusi signora, dove si trova la villa di Hadriano?" (Excuse me ma'am, where is Hadrian's villa?)

We're focusing on Spanish in this book in the "how to teach yourself section," but the various stories occur in different languages, as you've noticed. This is jumping ahead a little but merits the mention now.

Once you've learned Spanish, you can pick up closely related Italian and Portuguese with just a bit of effort. The phrase above is just about understandable to you if you already know Spanish.

Back to the story.

Young Italian women tend to avoid talking to male tourists, especially one-on-one. Perhaps consorting with strangers casts aspersions upon their virtue. Perhaps young Italian women are taught to suspect motives of marauding Americans. Perhaps talking is considered flirting, and flirting marks you as a "fallen woman." Who knows?

But at least this tourist speaks her language. There is that.

And here, in this setting, with no one around to see the exchange, and the wire fence keeping danger at bay, maybe, maybe just this once, the world will not end if she talks with the tourist. She can throw caution to the wind and talk to this tourist, one-on-one, on her porch in Capri, because he *does* speak Italian after all. How bad can he be?

"Questa e la via al Arco Naturale," she says. (This is the way to the Natural Arch.) Then she leans against her broom in a kind of Natural Arch of her own, a spectacular natural formation in her own right.

"Il Arco Naturale e *anche* molto bello." (The Natural Arch is *also* quite beautiful.)

She smiles and sends a look that speaks volumes.

"You think that Natural Arch is beautiful, you ain't seen nuthin' yet."

"Who needs Hadrian's Villa when you're packin' what I'm packin'?"

"Aren't you glad you got lost here?"

The tourist's mouth turns to cotton, his knees to jelly. The mountainous, rocky Isle of Capri has turned into one gigantic Sta-Puft marshmallow. Angels might be fluttering their wings nearby, for the tourist seems to have died and made a bee-line to heaven.

In movies, the fence would fall down and who knows what would happen next.

But alas, this is real life, not a Hollywood script. The fence stays, the woman undoes her leaning against the broom, and gets back to sweeping. Her eyes go back down to her porch.

"Grazie." (Thanks.)

"Ciao," she says without looking up.

He moves on. Oh, but that look, just for that second there.

"Il Arco Naturale e *anche* molto bello."

Cool things happen.

Not that anything happened, but there was that brief moment of "what if."

Doesn't always turn out even that good though. Even the most intrepid linguist discovers that "cool things may happen when you speak a foreign language", but that does not by any stretch guarantee that Cupid's arrows will fly. So this next one will have to go under the "embarrassing things also happen when you speak a foreign language."

Southern Portugal sports a beautiful beach scene. Sandy beaches, nice waves off the Atlantic, and lots of cliffs. Dress on the beach is certainly…European.

"Boa tarde," the hopeful tourist says. (Good afternoon.)

Next to him stands a woman, waist-deep in water, in the European mode of swimwear.

("Surely she will view me as something out of the ordinary," the tourist thinks to himself. "I've gone through the trouble of learning Portuguese, not exactly a mainstream European language.")

"Boa tarde," she responds.

She is not burdened with bad looks.

("Perhaps she is smitten with me", the tourist's fevered imagination flames on. "My command of the lingo marks me as more than just on ogling oaf, bent on satisfying my own animal cravings." Never mind that, at that moment, he WAS an ogling oaf, bent on satisfying his animal cravings.)

The conversation weaves from the weather to life at *universidade* (university, but you probably figured that one out on your own) to the wonderfulness of the beach.

("I sense she's about to throw herself at me. We may rock these nearby cliffs down to mere rubble with our fantastical goings-on. Oh joy, rapture! And all this, due to me being Master and Commander of Portuguese lingo. Oh, but the doors of ecstasy are opened by this wizardry with languages!")

She turns, she, of the European swim apparel, she of the not-burdened with bad looks, she, the promise of all things carnal, and speaks.

"O teu accento e muito comico." (Your accent is very comical.)

With that verbal smack down, she exits the water, wraps up in a towel, and walks away.

The tourist, the ogling oaf, the "Master and Commander of the Portuguese patois", is left in the water. Left with his fast-melting fantasy, left with his lonesome, and left with his "accento muito comico."

Sobering things happen when you speak (in this case, *comically* speak) foreign languages.

Cupid's arrows stayed sheathed on this trip.

Don't run off, though. More Portuguese is coming around the track.

Chapter 13

Mozambique Running: Portuguese

Atlanta is earning its nickname, Hotlanta. It's 9AM in June, and the rubberized running track on the Emory campus is already mushy from the heat. Heat waves shimmy from the bright orange oval, the white lines that separate lanes seem to squirm – long white snakes that want to wriggle off into the shade. Only mad dogs and Englishmen go out in the midday sun. A few morning joggers and weekend warriors are out in the midmorning sun today in Atlanta, Hotlanta.

In the center of the track is a natural grass field, serving double duty as a football and a soccer field. Conflicting chalk marks delineate end-zones, the box in front of the goals. Here a 50 yard line, there and out of bounds soccer line. The grass holds the memory of night time cool and clings to a smidgeon of dew. Better to stretch out here than on the petro-track.

Stretch, don't bounce. Stretch and hold it, hold it, hold it. An ounce of stretch is worth a pound of Ben-Gay. Stretch and hold it, hold it.

On the grass, stretching, a recent Med School graduate enjoys the last few weeks before internship. Once internship starts, might be hard to carve out a 9AM workout. Better run for fun now. It'll be a run all over the hospital, day and night, in a few weeks.

Stretch, don't bounce. Hold it, hold it. The last of the dew is going up in invisible smoke. Internship starts soon.

Internship - sun not yet up when going into the hospital. Sun already down when coming out of the hospital. No risk of sunburn there. Internship - linoleum floor below and a fluorescent bulb above.

But right now, it's still the green grass below and the blue hot sky above. Stretch, don't bounce.

Sweat now, fluoresce later.

On the track, zipping past the joggers, two blurs of bright green with Moçambique printed on the legs.

"Who are those guys?" the intern-to-be asks. He's stretching with another soon-to-be fluorescing Med School graduate.

"That's the Mozambique Olympic Team," the second stretcher says. "I read about it in the newspaper."

"Mozambique has an Olympic Team?"

"Yeah. There's a couple other African teams here."

A half dozen athletes in bright red sweats and another team in blue are also working out on the track. Chiseled in granite, they are, and unfathomably fast as they fly around the track.

"Zambia, I think, and some other team from there. I don't know, Tanzania or something like that."

"Why are they here?" the first intern asks.

"Getting ready for the Los Angeles Olympics. Turns out the track surface here at Emory is the same as the track surface in LA. So Emory said they could come here and practice."

The Mozambique team is doing a sprint exercise now, lifting their knees high up in the air. A rope ladder is lying on the track and they hop, hop, hop from space to space in the ladder. The whole team is glistening with sweat. They're all so thin their cheeks look sunken in.

None of the amateur joggers and Emory people are talking to the Olympic teams. And the African teams aren't talking to each other. So there's a little clump of green in one area, red in another, blue in another.

Here and there, a few coaches hold whistles and stopwatches. They shout out things in different languages.

The African Olympians stand out like peacocks against the backdrop of the Atlanta people wearing sweat-soaked T-shirts, baggy running shorts, some tank tops. Some are thin and pretty buffed. Others are suffering from heavy biscuit poisoning and ooze over their beltlines.

Three of the Mozambicans have taken off their shirts. 6-pack abdomens, long-thin arms (no pole vaulters or shot putters here), and legs that look like anatomic charts. From across the field you could trace the origin and insertion of all their leg muscles.

"Wouldn't it be cool to talk to them?" the second intern says.

"Yeah, how many Olympic athletes have you talked to in your life?"

"They must speak some weird African language, huh?" the second intern asks. "Zulu or Swahili or something."

"They might." The first intern says. "But the ones from Mozambique might speak something a little closer to home." He gets up from his stretching, shorts damp from the dewy grass. "I'm going to check this out."

The first intern goes over to the Mozambique team. Yes, they probably speak some impossible native African language. But that small, skinny country in the southeast section of Africa used to be a colony of Portugal. Twenty or so years ago, the country had thrown the colonials out and embarked on the wobbly road to independence that so many other African nations had. Civil war, massacre, Marxist dictators, playing off aid from East and West – independence with all the trimmings. Somehow, up from the gunsmoke and blood-drenched soil, they have raised a half dozen world-class athletes. The intern takes a chance that they speak Portuguese.

"Bom dia, bem-vindo aos estados unidos." (Good morning, welcome to the United States.)

The Mozambique athletes and coaches look over this stranger. Who in Atlanta speaks Portuguese? And how did this guy know to *speak* Portuguese? Who is this fellow that falls out of the Atlanta sky, lands at the practice track, and takes it upon himself to welcome them to America in their native (if adopted from the colonials) language?

But until then, the Mozambicans have had no way to talk to any Americans. All the way over here, but no language bridge to the Americans.

Now there is.

Great opportunity for the intern too. How often would he be able to talk to Olympic caliber athletes? How often would he be able to talk to people native to Mozambique? What was it like over there? How had they trained? Where did they live? Were they going to college?

The Portuguese isn't perfect. It is the second language for the athletes, and they speak it with a Mozambique accent! And Portuguese is a foreign language to the intern too, not his "best" second language by any stretch.

So they stumble and goof up and butcher a few phrases.

And they become friends.

Internship, with its murderous hours and its endless call nights under the fluorescent lights, is still a little ways off. So the intern comes back to the track a few times, strikes up a friendship, invites them over for dinner. But there's a little trouble in linguistic paradise. The coach does not like this budding warmth between his team and the Portuguese-speaking American. Directions from the Mozambique Marxist government are: no one "goes over to the capitalists."

No defections.

Just like the Russian sailors in the Smithsonian.

So, they can't come over for dinner. Doesn't prevent the intern from bringing a batch of chocolate chip cookies over to them. They're staying in some empty dorms on the Emory campus and give him a warm welcome (even if the coach does not) when he brings the cookies by.

A week passes and it's time for the team to head to Los Angeles. They give the intern a little token of Mozambique, a little carved wooden African mask. They've learned a few phrases in English from the intern.

"Thank you" they say.

"Boa sorte nos Olimpicos," the intern says.

Internship starts, but the intern is able to break away long enough to see the opening ceremonies on TV.

"Mozambique!" the announcer says as the teams file into the Los Angeles Olympic Stadium. The six athletes in their bright green uniforms march in, the one in front holding the flag. There's a brief close-up of the team members, and the intern remembers which ones took the most cookies. The coach is there too. He didn't take any cookies.

The intern isn't able to watch much of the games, isn't able to see any of the Mozambicans in action. In the paper, he is able to follow the medal totals for all the countries, though.

Mozambique: Gold–0, Silver–0, Bronze–0.

OK, none of them break the tape. None stand on the medal podium. None watch their flag raised, hold their hands over their hearts, and sing their national anthem. But they are all there. They are all a part of it. They are all Olympians.

And they all spoke Portuguese with the intern.

Mozambique has another civil war, and letters to the athletes go unanswered. What happens to the athletes, the intern never finds out.

Not every language adventure involves Olympic athletes and international intrigue.

Sometimes language adventures spring from looking at the title of a book and wondering, "Where did that title come from?"

Chapter 14

All Quiet on the Western Front: **German**

On the roof of St Peter's Basilica in Vatican City, Rome. Marble statues dating back to the Renaissance stand in a row, facing the great square of St Peter's. Behind the statues, a broad flat walkway. A few dozen tourists are walking around up there, peeking down to the square, squeezing between the statues.

The languages up there span the globe.

"Koko ni shashin o torite." (Take a picture over here.) Two Japanese tourists line, up, get their picture taken by a third, then they keep switching around until they've all gotten in the picture.

Two blond college age kids lean back on their outstretched arms, getting the sun full on their face. They have a guidebook open by their side, *Guidbok*. (Guidebook – maybe Swedish, maybe Norwegian?) Americans are there too, pointing and looking at their own guidebooks. And there's a group of Germans there, listening to their tour guide telling the story of Romulus and Remus, founders of Rome. He points to the seven hills of Rome (though, from up here, Rome looks like it has a hundred hills, hills everywhere). Then he points the other way, into the lush green gardens of the Vatican, acres of perfectly maintained walking paths. A tennis court peeks through a row of tall, narrow pine trees. Funny to think of a pope or a cardinal playing tennis.

One of the Germans, another college-age guy, drifts away from the Romulus and Remus lecture and steps to the dizzying edge of the walkway. A four foot wall separates him from a 150 foot drop to St. Peter's Square. An American points to the marble statues which are also leaning over that 150 foot precipice.

"Siehst du das?" (Do you see this?) the American asks in

German.

"Was?" (What?) the German asks.

The American points to wires, holding the statues in place. The wires are rusty and crumbling. There are cracks everywhere in the marble. The statues look as if they could snap – either marble cracking or wires snapping – and fall on the heads of the people 150 feet below.

"Sie konnen fallen. Und dann, nach unten, sie konnen fallen." (They could fall, and then, down below, they could fall.) the American says. The use of "fallen" is a play on words, for "fallen" means "to fall", as in English, and it also means "to fall down dead" as when soldiers are killed in battle. Germans say, "Er ist im Zweiten Weltkrieg gefallen." (He fell in World War II.) We say it when we're evoking a poetic sense – "In the fields of Gettysburg were our gallant fallen." So the American is saying, "The statues could fall and splatter the people down below", but trying to be a bit more poetic about it.

The German gets it right away.

By now the tour guide has broken off from his Romulus and Remus–o–rama and walked over by the statues too.

"Du sprichst Deutsch, oder?" (Do you speak German?) He tacks on a verbal hiccup common to German, putting "oder" (or) on the end of a sentence. So he actually said, "You speak German, or?"

"Ja, ich spreche Deutsch, oder." (Yes, I speak German, or.) The "oder" doesn't belong there, since it's an answer, but the American puts in there on purpose, just for grins.

The college student gets that too, and laughs. Not so the guide. The guide is looking over the American, but can't figure the accent. Something about how the "r" is pronounced. French and German (few people know this) have the exact same "r" sound. French has the reputation of this "gargly 'r'", but German has the exact same thing. Usually, when Americans pronounce the German "r", they say it the American way, and it's a dead giveaway.

The "r" is always the giveaway.

"Vous etes français?" (You are French – in French), the German guide asks.

"Non." (No – in French), the American says.

"Aus Kanada?" (From Canada – back in German.)

"Nein." (No – also back in German.)

This is too much fun. You never want to be pegged by your accent as where you're from. That means you have got a "thick American accent." Always better to be thought of as "from somewhere else?"

A mental Rolodex is flipping through the German tour guide's head. Not French, not French Canadian (damn, that "r" sounded so French).

"Nederlands." (Dutch?) The Dutch are great linguists.

"Nein."

Flocks of pigeons jump up from the square below, fly in a choreographed arc half way up to the level of the statues, and then swing back down to the square. Around the tour guide, some of his German flock gather.

"Ich bin ein Berliner." (I am a Berliner – more on this later), the American says, echoing the words of John F Kennedy at the Berlin Wall. This too, is an inside joke on the German language. Although JFK *thought* he was saying it right, he should have said, "Ich komme aus Berlin." (I come from Berlin.) "Berliner" is a term the Germans use for a particular kind of donut – a jelly donut if you must know. So, when JFK was standing at the, then, brand new Berlin Wall, he took this momentous and historical occasion to tell the entire world, teetering on the brink of World War III, "I am a jelly donut!"

The kids in the tour group all get this in a split second and start to giggle. Even the icy tour guide has to crack a little on this one.

"Na ja, mach nichts. Ich komme aus Amerika." (Naw, forget that, I'm from America – using lots of slangy German)

Now the tour guide shifts into English, no doubt for the

benefit of the benighted American.

"But no Americans speak German! Americans don't speak anything but English!"

"Entschuldigen Sie bitte." (Pardon me, please – using formal forms of address.) "Ich hatte vergessen." (I had forgotten.)

This is one of the golden moments of language-ness. Just proving that we Americans are NOT so bad at languages, showing them that we not only know the grammar and the vocabulary, but some of the intricacies, subtleties, and historical tidbits of the lingo.

-"Fallen" meaning "to fall" (like the statues were about to) as well as "to die" (like the unlucky people in the square were about to, should the statues fall).

-"Ich bin ein Berliner." That jelly donut thing is too much. On the History Channel, any show on the Cold War shows the dashing young president from "America's Camelot" standing up to this big, bad Commies. And he makes his dramatic stand at THE symbol of the Cold War. And to American ears, that "Ich bin ein Berliner" makes sense, even if you don't know much German. So to know the jelly donut implication is just plain fun.

The fun of language. Up on that roof, with that German guide trying to figure out where I was from, that was just too much fun.

Fun, the happiness of discovering a subtle shade of meaning, is one of the cool things that happens when you speak a foreign language. It's like solving a crossword or a Sudoku puzzle.

Not all fun moments occur in such dramatic settings. Sometimes, the fun comes when you're sitting in a chair, looking at a book, wondering about the title.

All Quiet on the Western Front.

Just how did they come up with the title?

Erich Maria Remarque wrote this classic anti-war novel

in German. He follows a classroom of German students who join the army at the outbreak of World War I. Glory and honor and flag waving turn into mud and lice and terror and dying in misery. The crucial sentence, the one that gave the book its title, comes at the end of the book.

The protagonist, Paul, has beaten all the odds and survived until the last days of the war. Bullets, shells, and poison gas have killed off everyone else, and he's the last one standing. Then...

"Er fiel an einem Tag der so still und ruhig war an den ganzen Front, das der Heeresbericht sich auf dem Satz beschrankte: Im Westen sei Nichts Neues zu melden."

("He fell on a day that was so still and peaceful on the entire front, that the High Command limited its report to once sentence: *In the west, nothing new to report.*")

Wait a minute! There's a disconnect here.

When you read a *translation* of that sentence, it says, "He fell on a day that was so still and peaceful on the entire front, that the High Command limited its report to one sentence: *All quiet on the Western Front.*"

Flip back to the cover of the German original:
Im Westen Nichts Neues. (*In the West, Nothing New*).
Look at the English title:
All Quiet on the Western Front.
Huh?

How did the translator get *All Quiet on the Western Front* from *In the West, Nothing New*?
Herein lies a tale. And *within* the tale lies a tale.

There is an Italian saying, "Traduttori, tradittori." (Translators, traitors – there's only one letter difference between the words in Italian.) The translators task is, on the surface, a piece of cake. You take the words from one language, and carry them across to the other language. Even the Latin says it:

Translate comes from the Latin "translatio" which is the past participle of "transferrere," meaning, to carry across.

So, let's do two examples in Spanish, since that's what we're concentrating on elsewhere.

You want to translate "the woman", you *carry across* the meaning and you get "la mujer." Easy.

You want to translate, "I'm going to the store," you *carry across* the meaning and you get "Voy a la tienda."

So how come the translator for *All Quiet on the Western Front* didn't just *carry across* the words *Im Westen Nichts Neues* and give us *In the West Nothing New*?

He didn't do it because a translator is more than that.

He didn't do it because language is more than that.

Language is not just sounds and words becoming "the woman" and "I'm going to the store." Language is poetry that makes you ache and song lyrics that make you cry. Language sets the mood, the atmosphere, the pulse of the everyday and the once in a lifetime. Language is:

-"Oh, the humanity!" when the Hindenberg lights up the evening sky and falls to earth.

-"That's one small step for a man. One giant leap for mankind." when the whole world holds its breath and watches a grainy image of a man uniting us all for, maybe, the last time ever.

-"Ein Volk! Ein Reich! Ein Deutschland!" (One people, one kingdom, one Germany) when a madman whips a Nuremberg crowd into a murderous frenzy and plunges the whole globe into darkness.

-"Why don't you come up sometime and see me?" when Mae West says everything that needs saying with her one raised eyebrow.

-"We have struck an iceberg."

-"This just in, Kennedy has been shot."

-"There's a report from New York of a fire at the Twin Towers.

157

Earlier, a plane…"

Language has an emotional tug, a yanking at the heartstrings, that proves elusive to *carry across*. Translators do their best, and do a great job, most of the time. But there's always an element of the "traitor" (tradittore) to the "translator" (traduttore) because you haven't always got such an easy target. Not everything is "la mujer is how you say 'the woman'" and "Voy a la tienda is how you say 'I'm going to the store'.

How do you convey the panic and horror of the radio announcer at seeing the Hindenberg? "O, la humanidad!" in Spanish is the direct translation, but it sounds clunky.

"Eso es un paso por un ser humano, un paso gigante para todos los humanos." That comes across pretty well, actually, though you could translate it a few different ways.

Sometimes translators make a different mistake, *improving* on the original. Isn't that more like *editing* than translating? And is that what the translator of *All Quiet on the Western Front* did?

Let's dig a little deeper and see where that came from. Others have made the same speculation I'm going to lay out. (Wikipedia itself came up with the same explanation I did, though I'd like to think I thought of it first.)

What was the setting of the translation?

The original came out in the 1920's, as did the translation. At that time, America's Civil War was still relatively "close" in the country's collective memory. 1860's America is to the 1920's as 1940's America is to today.

The Civil War was to the translator what World War II is to us.

Civil War era songs were still being played in the 1920's. In a similar vein we still listen to some songs from the 40's after all (at Big Band dances and stuff you'll hear Tommy Dorsey and Benny Goodman songs).

And one Civil War song MAY have influenced the translator

of *All Quiet on the Western Front* and given us this most haunting of titles.

All Quiet Along the Potomac is a song about a single soldier, not an important general or anything, shot dead while on duty. It doesn't make the news, is not a part of some epic battle, and does not bring fame or glory to anyone. It's just one person dying on an otherwise quiet day.

> *"All quiet along the Potomac," they say.*
> *Except now and then a stray picket*
> *Is shot as he walks on his beat to and fro,*

The same idea comes across in the final scene of *All Quiet on the Western Front*. In both versions of the movie, Paul is shot by a French sniper as he reaches out to touch a butterfly (the 1930 version) and to look at a bird (the 1970 made-for-TV version). Nothing of a sniper is mentioned in the book, it simply says "He fell on a day", so it could have been anything that killed him. But the notion of one "insignificant" loss set against the backdrop of an enormous conflict is still there.

Trivia about the song itself; as was characteristic of a lot of events in the Civil War, "both sides" are represented. The words were written by a Northerner, Ethel Lynn Beers, in 1861. The music for it was written by a Southerner, John Hill Hewitt, in 1863. So blue and gray can both lay claim to *All Quiet Along the Potomac*.

So picture the translator, staring at the German original.

> *"Er fiel an einem Tag der so still und ruhig war an den ganzen Front, das der Heeresbericht sich auf dem Satz beschrankte: Im Westen sei Nichts Neues zu melden."*

And he draws on his command of German to render a word-for-word translation:

He fell on a day that was so still and peaceful on the entire front, that the High Command limited its report to once sentence: *In the west, nothing new to report.*

But something sticks in his craw. *In the west, nothing new,* just doesn't cut it. But that's what the author said! Those are his words! But that's not his meaning. That's not his essence. There's more to this than just "In the west, nothing new."

There's innocence lost.

There's an entire classroom of idealistic students torn to shreds or riddled with bullets or drowning in the mud or crushed by a caved-in dugout. And there's one guy who has avoided the bullets and pulled himself out of the mud and dug himself out of the cave-in and made it to this, the 11th hour of the war. And then, he dies. The one life he has, the one life he has hung onto through 1001 perils, is snuffed out, just like that. And it's such a non-event that is doesn't even merit a line, a word, in any official report.

How do I translate that? How do I *carry across* that idea?

In the next room, someone is plunking a tune on the piano and singing the words of *All Quiet Along the Potomac.* They're on the last part of the last verse.

> *All quiet along the Potomac tonight,*
> *No sound save the rush of the river;*
> *While soft falls the dew on the face of the dead—*
> *The picket's off duty forever.*

That's it.

The picket on duty by the river becomes Paul on duty in the trenches. The death of one man in the Civil War becomes the death of one man in The Great War. (As World War I was called in the 1920's.)

The sentence "Im Westen sei Nichts Neues zu melden" becomes "All Quiet on the Western Front." And the title is born.

But was the *traduttore* a *traditore*?

Did the translator exceed his calling, did he improve on the original? Did he make something "not so haunting" into something unforgettable? Only a German would know, because only a German really knows what "Im Westen Nichts Neues" means.

The answer is surprising.

On the roof of St Peter's Basilica in Vatican City, Rome. Marble statues dating back to the Renaissance stand in a row, facing the great square of St Peter's. Behind the statues, a broad flat walkway. A few dozen tourists are walking around up there, peeking down to the square, squeezing between the statues.

The American has shaken up a group of German tourists, especially their tour guide, by speaking to them in their own tongue. He's even pulled a few linguistic rabbits out of his hat by making references to the double-meaning word "fallen" and by quoting John F Kennedy's famous donut line.

He has to ask them because he has to know, what is the deal with *Im Westen Nichts Neues*? What's the German take on the title, the translation to *All Quiet on the Western Front*, and the general idea that the translation is *more* than the original. So often the translation loses something, and is somehow *less* than the original. But this time, to English-speaking ears anyway – well – what do the Germans think?

"Nein, zu uns ist es besser wenn man 'Im Westen Nichts Neues' sagt," (No, to us it's better when you say "In the west, nothing new.") says the tour guide. The German tour guide is now mollified and convinced that, yes, there is the occasional American who *can* speak German.

He explains something that the English speakers don't grasp - what "the West" has always meant to the Germans.

When Rome was bent on conquering the world, their legions attacked Germany from *the west*, along the Rhine river (Germany's western border). France, Germany's traditional rival, has always been a lurking presence in *the west*. World War I had an eastern front (against Russia) and a western front (against

France, Britain, and, later, America), but it was *the west* where most of the fighting occurred.

So, from the west, there's always something.

From the west, there's threat, there's war, there's death.

Across the Rhine, to the west, you might see dust rising from approaching legionnaires, from French artillery.

From the west comes a telegram that your father is fallen, your husband, your brother.

In the West, Something New. This has been the call sign for disaster.

In the West, Something New. This can only be bad news.

In the West, Nothing New. Aah. At last, a quiet day. Nothing's wrong.

Paul, the fictional Paul of *All Quiet on the Western Front*, must be safe.

There was someone *else* out there on the Western Front. This person was real, not fictitious. This person was my grandfather, and his German was about to be put to the test.

Chapter 15

A Cellar in France, 1918: German

Learning German is part of one American doctor's training in 1917. A lot of the medical literature is in German. To keep up, you learn German. This 28 year old native Minnesotan has also used his German speaking with the German immigrant farmers who live and work around the area. When they come into the hospital, he's able to take their histories.

Not so good speaking with the Swedes and Norwegians that come in. Maybe someday the doctor will pick that up as well.

But things take a turn in 1917 when America declares war on Germany, and the doctor, just finishing his internship, volunteers to enter "The War to End All Wars." America does not yet have much of an army, but it does have a small army of doctors, willing to go "Over There" right away and fill the depleted ranks of the British Army's medical corps.

Might get a chance to use that German, though, as a doctor, he doesn't feel he'll get close enough to hear it spoken. He *hopes* he doesn't get near enough to hear it spoken.

He does.

It's now a March evening, 1918, and the Germans are pushing the British back, back, back, in a tremendous offensive. They're attempting to win the war before America's troops (now arriving in France by the thousands) can tilt the balance against Germany.

The Minnesota doctor is caught in his adopted Army's retreat. He's been serving with the British for the last 5 months and is now a front line medical officer. He is in the small town of Marcelcave, France. He is in charge of a cellar full of wounded British soldiers, 19 in all. (One of the wounded men will kill himself, unable to endure the pain of his wounds, that same night.) The doctor is taking care of these men, who are too seriously wounded to evacuate.

He steps out of the cellar to get a breath of fresh air. His journal relates:

> *Flares went up to the west, indicating the town was cut off.*

(The Germans were firing flares to indicate their positions. Escape was to the west, the same direction from which the flares shot up.)

> *It is said, 'Once to every man and nation comes the moment to decide' and this surely was my moment. Could I get away in the gathering darkness and escape capture. Or worse. Could I leave the men who were crying to me for help.*
>
> *The answer came fast and easy, and I have never made a decision that I was so sure was right. Like a flash from a clear sky I knew. I could no more leave these men than I could cut off my own hand.*
>
> *I went into the cellar and lit a candle for light.*

Hours later, the German bombardment of the town stops.

> *Suddenly it fell quiet. This aroused my curiosity for why should they do this but that they were entering the town themselves.*

The Germans are advancing fast and "cleaning up the town" as quickly as possible so they can move on.

> *From far away, we heard a steady progression of sounds. A muffled 'whoomp' followed by a kind of 'whooshing' noise. Closer and closer it was coming. I hadn't heard the*

'whooshing' sound before so asked one of the wounded men what it meant. He had one of those Cockney accents that take some getting used to.

"'Ey's cleanin' out da cella's. First it's a grenade, you see, to keep ev'ryone back. Then it's the flame throweh. 'At's what's makin' da second soun'. It's an a'ful thing it is, suh."

The doctor is now getting his chance to hear German. From up the street, he can hear the sequence, the teamwork, of the German mopping-up squad.

I could hear them now.

"Hans, los!" then there's be a clicking sound that I took to be the pulling of the fuse on the grenade, then a few seconds later, 'Whoomp', sometimes a few shots being fired. Then there would be another clicking, which I took to be pressing some triggering device on the flamethrower. Then there would be the 'Whoosh' sound.

As they came closer, they were surprisingly noisy, stepping on broken glass and timbers from the ruined town as they went.

I thought of home, and how the news would be received. Mother would take it hard, and my brothers. Odd how the medical training had a way of hitting at that time. There wouldn't be much of me to send home. They probably wouldn't even find me, or if they did, they certainly wouldn't recognize me.

I supposed it would hurt, though how much and for how long was beyond my ken. I somehow didn't feel that me going would be a terrible loss, one doctor more or less in this great war where so many had already gone before. But the men in the cellar with me. Them going somehow struck me as the real tragedy. What would their mothers do? Their wives and sweethearts.

The Germans approach the door to his cellar, the team crunching and snapping their way up to the entrance.

"Hans", the German officer was shouting to the man who, from earlier shouts, seemed to be the man holding the grenades. In a few seconds, there would be a click, then the grenade, then the second click and that whooshing sound.

So the great mystery was about to be revealed to me. In a kind of absent way, I wondered if the grenade or the flames would take me there.

Another crunching footstep then a loud crash, a second voice (maybe Hans?) shouted "Verdammt!." Hans had apparently slipped and fallen.

When I heard him say that, and I understood him – he had said, "Damn it!", something occurred to me that I have always been thankful for.

"Halt!" I shouted, with all my strength. "Halt! Verwundeten hier! Nicht werfen, bitte. Englische Soldaten hier, und ein amerikanischer Arzt!"

(Stop! Stop! Wounded here. Don't throw please. English soldiers here and an American doctor!)

In the second before Hans was going to throw that grenade in among us, a thought occurred to me. If I speak to them in their language, they just might take a second to consider their actions.

It's one thing to kill a nameless enemy who can't even talk to you. But it's rather a different thing when they are asking for mercy in your Mother Tongue.

It remained quiet at the top of the stairway. In my imagination, I saw some ferocious Teutonic warriors, poised to hurl death on our heads. But by their pausing, I knew they had heard me. They must be thinking.

There was no clicking sound, and a short time later, poking his way down the stairs, crouching so low his head was almost at his ankles, a German soldier came down, pistol first. His face was dirty and smudged, but so young as to have never seen a razor on it. He came in, straightened up, looked around, took in our situation, and held out his hand to me.

"Amerikaner? Was zum Teufel machen Sie hier?" (An American? What the hell are you doing here?)

It worked. The Germans heard their own language spoken, and they held off on throwing those grenades down into the cellar.

Knowing a language can save your life. It saved my Grandpa's.

Chapter 16

Cutting Loose and Having a Little Fun with Languages

Languages aren't *always* a matter of life and death.

There's *just plain fun* to be had as you learn about languages too.

Learning a language is work, no doubt. The books that say "Estonian Made Easy" and "Inuit in 10 Minutes a Day" are a shade optimistic. You face a modicum of "nose to the grindstone" if you're going to become a linguist.

But! No reason we can't take a little time out from our studies and see what fun lies inside all these languages! Put down your Dictaphone, let the *201 Spanish Verbs* book chill out for a while, and put your feet up. We'll look at tongue twisters, weird links to English, history, French cuisine, proverbs, four-syllable sayings in Chinese, anything that looks interesting.

Nothing educational here, this is linguistic goofing off! Party like a rock star!

SPANISH

First, some tongue twisters.

(Try saying these 10 times fast.)

Tres tristes tigres trillaron trigo en un trigal.
(Three sad tigers threshed wheat in a wheatfield.)

Yo no compro coco.
Porque como poco coco, poco coco compro.
(I don't buy coconut.
Because I eat little coconut, little coconut do I buy.)

El otorrinolaringologo de Pranguricutirimicuaro se quiere

Desotorrinolaringoparangaricutirimicuarizar porque si no
Desotorrinolaringoparangaricutirimicuazara lo van a
Desotorrinolaringologoparangaricutirimicuarizar.

(The ENT doctor in Parangaricutirimicuaro wants to
stop practicing in Parangaricutirimicuaro because if he stops
practicing in Parangaricutirimicuaro, then they will make him
stop practicing in Parangaricutirimicuaro.)

One thing you will notice between "Castilian" Spanish
(spoken in Spain) and "New World" Spanish (spoken everywhere
else) is the pronunciation of the "c" and the "z." In "New World"
Spanish, the "c" and the "z" are pronounced like an "s." In Spain,
they pronounce these "th" as in "think." But in Spain, they can
still pronounce the "s" sound, because they pronounce "s" like
"s"! So, "seis" (six) in Castilian Spanish is "seis", not "theith."

In Mexico City, cerveza (beer) is pronounced SER-VAY-
SAH.

In Madrid, cerveza is pronounced THER-VAY-THAH.

To the person who's spoken "New World" Spanish all along,
a trip to Madrid can trigger a frantic "switch to Castilian."
As you're formulating your sentences, you try desperately to
"anticipate" the c's and z's and form up your th's on the fly.

Not so hard to *understand*. (Receiving)

Can be hard to *transmit*. (Sending)

So a college student in Madrid is trying to make a good
impression, throwing in "th" every time a "c" or "z" appears. But
he fumbles, and makes the Castilians crack up at the bar.

"Dame una cerveza" (give me a beer). Trouble is, he
anticipates the "c" but forgets the "z", ends up pronouncing it
THER-VAY-SAH. Half Castilian, half New World.

No harm done, everyone understands everything, and the
Madrileños even pay for the mispronounced beer.

ITALIAN

The Italian Army hasn't kicked much butt of late. But from a linguistic standpoint, the success of their predecessor, the Roman Legions, is nothing short of fantastic. Google the Roman Empire at its peak – from the north of England, west to Spain, the northern rim of Africa, east all the way to present day Romania (note the "roman" in Romania), back up into Europe, stopping more or less at the Rhine. And everywhere the Roman legions went, the Roman language, Latin, went.

The *linguistics* is a story known to one and all – Spanish, Portuguese, Romansch (a language of Switzerland), French, Italian (no kidding), and Romanian are all direct descendants of Latin. English and the Germanic languages are also influenced extensively by Latin, though not as much as Spanish and Italian. As noted in an earlier chapter, that makes life considerably easier for the budding linguist. Learn *one*, and you've got a gateway to *many*!

But the *history* of it begs one big question. How come the Romans conquered everyone? Sure, they were warriors, but come on! EVERYONE was a warrior back then. Those were tough times.

The Romans must have been doing something fundamentally *better* than everyone else, they must have had something *on* everybody else, a better *technique*, a better *something*.

What was it?

What did the Romans do that conquered the world (for them) and made learning a bunch of languages easier (for us)?

Look to the right.

Romans practiced, practiced, practiced, and when things got "up close and personal" they looked to the right.

What?

Romans advanced in tight columns, shields forming a solid wall as they advanced. Troops were armed with spears and short swords. When this wall of shields smashed into the enemy (and, as Rome expanded, *everyone* became their enemy), the Romans made the most of human nature and the most of their short swords.

Most people are right-handed, and when the barbarian line collided with the Roman line, the natural instinct was to raise the right arm to batter the enemy in front of them.

The Romans, our linguistic ancestors, didn't do that.

They kept their shields up, blocking the man in front of them, and they *looked to the right*, they looked to the vulnerable underarm area of the barbarian to their right. With an underarm jab, they'd nail the guy where he was wide open.

Tight discipline in battle, and a jab to the right. Bad news for the barbarian 2000 years ago, good news for linguists today. Funny how that works.

Let's jump from Latin to its great-great-grandchild, Italian, and see if those Romans have something more pleasant for us than a short sword in our side.

Long ago, Rome hung up its shield and sword and took up the monastic robe, leaving us these sayings:

"L'abito non fa il Monaco."
The cowl does not make the monk.

"Fra Modesto non fa mai priore."
Brother Modest never becomes the prior. A celibate version of our "Faint hearts win no fair maidens."

From monks to priests:

"Ogni prete loda le sue reliquie."
Each priest praises his own reliquary. Everyone blows their own horn.

"Non tutti possono andare a Roma a vedere il Papa."
Not everyone can go to Rome to see the Pope. We can't all be superstars.

171

If, by chance, you *did* get to Rome to see John Paul II, you had a chance to see a real linguistic superstar. In 1984, from about 100 feet away, I saw, and heard, the man in action. He reeled off prayers in a half dozen languages for an assemblage of about 50,000 people. His Polish accent came through in all the languages, but he said everything right! Blessings with all the language trimmings!

Speaking of blessings, Italians suffer through the "blessing" of relatives just as we do.

"Molti parenti, molti tormenti."
Many relatives, many torments.

"Val di piu un amico che cento parenti."
Better one friend than 100 relatives.

When beset by loving relatives with luggage in hand, a friendly reminder or two:

"Le migliori visite sone le piu breve."
The best visits are the shortest.

"Ospiti e pesce dopo tre giorni puzza."
Fish and visitors after three days stink. Wait a minute! Didn't Benjamin Franklin say that? Did HE get it from the Italians, or did the Italians take it from him?

As long as we're on malodorous subjects, let's take up with two highly respected professions, lawyers and doctors.

"Buoni avvocati sono cattivi vicini."
Good lawyers are bad neighbors.

"Gli errori dei medici la terra li copre."
Earth covers the doctor's errors.

So the descendants of the Roman empire see fit to "diss" docs and lawyers. Certainly, they must love and cherish the sacred institution of marriage.

"Chi ha moglie ha doglie."
Who has a wife has sorrows.

"Chi non ha moglie non ha padrone."
Who does not have a wife does not have a boss.

Ouch! Doubt the political correctness thought police will let that go. Someone in Italy must be making up "equivalent" sayings about husbands as we speak.

But, lest I dwell overly long on these Italian tidbits, I should take to mind:

"Ogni pazzo e savvio quando tace."
Each fool is wise when he shuts up.

'Nuf said!

FRENCH

Those French and their food! Rome created an Empire, Napoleon *almost* created an Empire, but French cooks have definitely conquered the world's kitchens. This fascination with food extends to their sayings.

"Va te faire un oeuf."
Go make an egg. Their version of "Get lost." We're presuming they're talking about *cooking* an egg and not *laying* one yourself.

Say you feel more strongly about this person, then you can "Donner le bouillon de onze heures", (give the 11 o'clock bullion), which means "To poison them." 11 o'clock is apparently the time you poison people in France. (Whether AM or PM is not specified, which means twice a day you have to keep your guard up if given bouillon in France.)

Maybe murder is not your cup of tea – "Ce n'est pas mes

oignons" (these are not my onions). You may still be accused of it! In that case, you have fallen "dans le petrin" (in the kneading trough) – which means you're in big trouble. This poisoning rap may be hard to beat, even if you are a big cheese (un grosse legume) – a big legume, so the cops will do what?

They will arrest you, and when it comes to questioning you closely, they will grill you (cuisiner) – cook. "Cuisiner" is how the French say "Give the 3rd degree."

There's no escaping these cooking expressions. What else awaits the person accused of giving the 11 o'clock bouillon?

Your lawyer will not "work for peanuts" (travailler pour des prunes) – work for prunes/plums, literally.

The judge may cut you a deal, and "promise you the moon" (promettre plus de beurre que de pain) – promise you more butter than bread.

You're case is dismissed! Hope you have some money left over. Make sure you "save some money for a rainy day" (garder une poire pour le soif) – save a pear for the thirst.

If you wait too long, then it's too late, and "the horse is already out of the barn" (C'est de la moutarde de après diner) – This is mustard after the dinner is over.

All these eggs and plums and mustard would work hell on anyone's innards.

Can't we ever get out of the kitchen?

No.

When marital discord erupts in a French household, the term used is "le torchon brule" (the dish towel is on fire). You can picture the scene.

Husband and wife are doing the dishes; husband informs wife of his infidelity (in France? Never!), wife gets so mad the dish towel in her hand bursts into flames.

Any French tongue-twisters before we finally give our overloaded stomachs a rest?

Le riz tenta le rat. Le rat tente tata le riz tentant.

The rice tempts the rat. The tempted rat touches the tempting rice.

Quand un gendarme me rie, dans la gendermarie, tous les gendarmes me rient, dans la gendarmerie.

When a policeman laughs at me in the police station, all the policemen laugh at me in the police station.

Diderot dinait du dos d'un dodo dindon.
Diderot dined on the back of a plump turkey.

Le ver vert va vers le verre vert.
The green grub does to the green grass.

Six sous ces saucissons-ci?
Six cents for these sausages?

When you hear these, especially in the kind of smooshed together way that French sounds anyway, it's too much.

Before we say "Au revoir" to France, we have to look at that sexy French accent. When a French person speaks English, their accent turns your knees to water. Ooh la la! Does it work the other way around? How does it sound to the French when WE speak French with our American accent?

I asked several French people. The universal response?

"Non! Ce n'est pas sexy de tout." (No! This is not sexy [they use the same word] at all!)

Sacre bleu!

GERMAN

Germany has had some, ahem, *memorable* leaders in its past. But he-who-people-prefer-not-to-mention has not made it into any set expressions in German. Instead, the Kaiser – Germany's version of the Latin Caesar – appears in a bunch.

"Kaiserwetter" (Kaiser's weather) means splendid weather.

Weather that is literally "fit for a king."

"Um des Kaisers Bart straiten" (Quarrel about the Kaiser's beard) carries the meaning, "Argue over useless details" or "Debate how many angels can dance on the head of a pin."

"Wo der Kaiser selbst geht allein" (Where the Kaiser himself goes alone) gets a little scatological. This refers to the bathroom.

When in a German-speaking area (Germany, Austria, parts of Switzerland, a few places in Belgium) the average American may feel more at home than when in the "Latinized" parts of Europe. Call it a feeling that's hard to prove. The Roman conquest stopped at the Rhine, so Germany had a *brush* with Romanization, rather than a complete covering of Roman occupation. And English is first a *Germanic* language, later a Latin one. The earliest invaders of Britain were Angles and Jutes from Northern Germany/Denmark, so that Germanic footprint goes way back. You see it in the most basic words:

Hand — Hand
Foot — Fuss
Arm — Arm
Father — Vater
Mother — Mutter
God — Gott

And you see it in the most basic expressions:

"Luegen haben kurze beinen." — Lies have short legs, the exact same as ours.

"Die Liebe macht blind." — Love makes blind, almost the same as our "Love is blind."

"Wer rastet, der rostet." — Who rests, rusts, same as ours.

The Romance languages are close cousins of ours. German is a brother. But they don't always go with us word for word, there's a little room for poetic interpretation.

"Der letzte Rock hat keine Taschen." — The last shirt has no pockets. Another way of saying, "You can't take it with you."

"Die Radieschen von unten betrachten." — Look at the little radishes from below. That's how a German "looks up at daisy roots."

But enough of this doom and gloom, what about the good times?

Germany's gone to war with France how many times? So you think they'd hold them in utter contempt. Not so? How does a German describe the "Life of Riley"?

"Wie Gott in Frankreich lebt." — How God lives in France. Must be pretty nice over there! Maybe we should invade them again and get in on some of that action.

RUSSIAN

Only the "mature" among us can remember doing our "Duck and Cover" drills. Presumably, a 50 megaton Soviet warhead, falling on Blessed Sacrament grade school's roof, would kill fewer of us if we had our desk between us and the thermonuclear fireball.

Their language can seem just as threatening – different alphabet, complex grammar, tons of weird endings to words, two different "types" of verbs. Ouch! It's enough to make you duck and cover under your desk again.

But you have to love a language that gives you this saying:

"Tomu, komu sooshdyena bit povyeshyennim, nye stoit boyatsya utonoot."
"Who is fated to hang, will never drown."

Those Russkis know how to have a good time.

Russian has homonyms just like we do. One word, same spelling, same sound, two different meanings. A few catch the eye:

"Pol" means *floor* or…uh…*sex*. If you can find a link there, good for you.

"Brak" means *defective goods* or *marriage*. If you can find a link there, keep your mouth shut around your spouse!

"Mir", especially given the history of the Cold War, has an especially interesting double meaning.

Mir means *peace* or *earth*. So, a hawk could say, "Ha! When the Russians say *peace*, what they're saying is, they want to take over the entire *earth*." The apologist for Russia could say, "They're not so bad, they want *peace* on *earth*." What **is** Russia thinking? Hard to say.

Russia hasn't just made our life tough, they've made it tough for their own people. People killed in bloody purges, sent by the millions to the snowy Gulags out in Siberia, this is one brutal country. This tough treatment has snuck into their sayings:

"Za odnovo beete, dvuk nyebeetikh dayut."

One beaten person is worth two non-beaten ones. (Ulp!) Quite a country, where getting beaten wins you admiration.

How could such a rugged country have such troubles? Did it have anything to do with the Russian work ethic? What do they say about work?

"Durakov rabota lyubeet."

Work loves fools. So the SMART people find a way of getting OUT of work. No wonder the USSR fell apart.

But they've said good bye to all that Soviet communism stuff, haven't they? Eeeek! Not if you listen to their national anthem. The music is the same as the national anthem of the USSR, music by Alexander Alexandrov. They "purged" some of the Soviet stuff (taking out mention of Lenin and Stalin; removing mention of an "Unbreakable Union" – it did break up, after all), but it's the same music.

It may be true that:

"Umom Rossee nye ponyat."
The soul of Russia cannot be understood.

Better keep that desk nearby in case you have to "Duck and Cover."

HEBREW

Talk about the ability to rebound. Hebrew spread across the globe along with the Jewish diaspora, but was spoken only during religious services for 2,000 years. Countless persecutions, pogroms, autos-da-fe, and banishments later, Hebrew resurfaces as a spoken language. One man spearheaded the effort, Eliezer Ben-Yahuda. How many people can claim that – reviving an entire language!

Hebrew uses Stealth technology to weave its way into our language. Keep your ears open for these colorful additions to English.

Chutzpah – Literally referring to the testicles. Means "nerve" or "gall." The classic definition of chutzpah is the man who shoots both his parents then throws himself at the mercy of the judge. "Judge, look at me, a poor orphan!" That is chutzpah.

Mazal (sometimes spelled mazel) tov. Good luck. Jews with no knowledge of Hebrew still know to say "Mazal tov" when they hear of good tidings. But this expression goes beyond "good luck." It's a congratulations to the lucky person (kid celebrating their Bar/Bat Mitzvah, couple on the birth of a child) but it's also congratulations to the bearer of the good tidings. It's congratulations and well wishes all around! So, at the Jewish wedding, it's "Mazal tov" to the bride, "Mazal tov" to the groom, to the parents, to the distant cousins, to the caterers, the busboys, the guys in the band. Mazal tov to everybody!

YIDDISH

It's a shame this language is disappearing. To look at it with the cold eye of the analytical linguist, this is a hybrid language of mostly German, some Russian, some Hebrew, a dash of Polish and tidbits of anything else you can think of. Spoken mostly in Eastern Europe and the first language for a huge number of Jewish immigrants, Yiddish is written in the Hebrew script.

If you speak German and watch a movie in Yiddish, you'll follow most of what's going on.

Alas, Yiddish is fading fast, doesn't really have a home anymore, and publications/theater/newspapers in this quaint language are not holding their ground.

But Yiddish has given us a few expressions that won't go away anytime soon. And more than that, it's given us an *intonation*, a way of speaking, that underlies countless stand up comics and actors.

Oy vay! (Oh, the pain!) This little gem can (and has been) inserted into a million settings:

"The IRS is on the phone and has some questions for me? Oy vay!"

"Dad, meet my new boyfriend, Viper. He says his tattoos are so good you can hardly tell they were put on in prison."
"Oy vay."

The Yiddish custom of saying a word, then making a rhyming second word, lends a piquancy to all kinds of verbal exchanges:

"Size schmize, I don't care how big the wedding cake is. As long as my daughter gets married to a doctor."

"Turtle schmurtle, I say that pet of yours is a pest and it's got to go!"

If some evil genius could slither into English and yank out all the Yiddish flavor, we'd be left with a pretty bland bowl of chicken soup.

What's the matter, you don't like my soup?

CHINESE

A word or two to the hardy linguist who takes on Chinese. Good luck.

We'll get into the fun stuff soon (that is, after all, the purpose of this chapter), but here's a little detour if you "go the Chinese route."

The Tough Stuff

1. Tones. The word "ma" can mean "mother, horse, scold, or rope" depending on whether your voice stays steady, rises, falls, or falls a little then rises, respectively.

2. The written language – little pictographs – is absolutely brutal. A *few* of the words "make sense", but other than that, you're in for some brutal memorizing if you decide to take on this baby.

The Good News

1. China is the up and coming economic powerhouse of the world as well as the 600 pound gorilla in the population department. You'll have people to practice with wherever you are and wherever you go.

2. Since Chinese is *so tough*, few people take it on, so when you DO make the effort, you get a lot of help and encouragement from Chinese people.

3. *And* (since Chinese is so tough), when you pull it

out of your hat at a cocktail party (see next chapter), you impress the living hell out of people. Impressing people! Your entire reason for living!

4. Chinese has simple grammar (some cosmic attempt at justice for their complex writing and tone system). You won't find yourself conjugating long lists of verb forms or invoking the God-forsaken subjunctive mood, ever.

5. In all the variants of the *Teach Yourself* books, they spell everything out phonetically, so you don't need to "know Chinese already" to learn it.

6. If you screw up the tones (most Americans say the second tone, over and over again, with little ability to hit the first, third, or fourth tones), the Chinese people listening to your garbled attempts will still be able to puzzle out what you're saying.

The Chinese Fascination with "Four"

The Chinese consider the number "four" unlucky, since the word "four" and the word "death" sound similar. They ARE the same sound (to our ears) but have different tones. If you go to a Chinese hospital, no room will have the number "4" in it.

But in a weird twist, the Chinese use four syllable *sayings* all the time. They're called "Chengyu." Four Chinese words strung together that "say more" than the four words. One of them comes directly into English.

Hao jiu bu jian – means "Long time no see." We translate that into, well, "long time no see." This gives you a little clue into the simple grammar structure. Just ideas, just little pictures strung together, and from this, you fill in the nuances.

"Gosh, what a shame we haven't seen each other in so long."
"My bad, I should have contacted you earlier."
"Your bad, *you* should have contacted me earlier."

All this is conveyed when you say "Long time no see."

Here's some more chengyu.

Bao sin jiu huo – Bring kindling douse fire. A sort of pre-hydrocarbon way of saying "Pouring gas onto the flames to put them out." You're attempting to do something good, but using the wrong method. In English this would be, "The road to hell is paved with good intentions."

Bei huan li he – Joy sorrow parting reunion. All of life in four little words! Not too different from Tevya's song in "Fiddler on the Roof:
To life! One day it's honey and raisin cakes, next day it's bellyaches. Drink Lechayim, to life!

Yi ri san qiu – One day, three years. Time crawls.

In a sick twist in history, China took this whole "four" business to absurd extremes. During the Cultural Revolution of 1966, Mao Tse Tung whipped up a frenzy of hyper-purist Communism. Anyone with the tiniest link to "the West" was imprisoned, lost their job, tortured, or killed. As Red Guards (mostly students) terrorized the country, they kept invoking the number four:

The Red Guard vowed to smash the "Four Old":
-Old thought.
-Old culture.
-Old customs.
-Old habits.

They cried out to Mao, who was the "Four Greats":
-Great leader.
-Great helmsman.
-Great commander.
-Great teacher.

And when some other Communist leaders were accused of trying to overthrow Mao, how many were there?

The Gang of Four.

Oy vay, enough of this four business. For we must remember this:

Guo you bu ji – Going beyond no good.

That means, enough is enough with Chinese. Let's jump across the narrow Sea of Japan to the Land of the Rising Sun and see what we can dig up there.

JAPANESE

To get a feel for just how foreign Japanese is, look at a map. An island country, but, unlike England, this island resisted invaders successfully. (England resisted valiantly, but succumbed damned near every time.) When you successfully resist an invasion, you get to keep your language. When you *unsuccessfully* resist an invasion, your language gets "coated" with the language of the invader. When you unsuccessfully resist many invaders, your language gets "multi-coated."

Not so Japan. They resisted invaders. They resisted "multi-coating" their language.

In their isolation, they've developed a language as complex as their social hierarchy – different verb forms depending on "where you are in the pecking order." Whereas Chinese grammar is "Me Tarzan, you Jane" simple, Japanese grammar is a tad more difficult.

Here's how you say "Me Tarzan, you Jane" in Japanese.

"As for me, Tarzan (humble form) is called; as for you (any one of 3 or 4 forms, depending on whether we are friends, workers, or lovers [!]), Jane is called (again, the verb forms vary depending on whether Jane and Tarzan share a workplace or a futon together!).

Yipes!

Any language flowering in such a curiously insular setting

must have some unique sayings. And indeed it does. Japanese fixed expressions are a gas.

We "get fired." In Japan, you "kubi ni naru" (become a neck). The visual here is – you become a neck that then gets stuck out and chopped off with a samurai sword. What a way to end your career.

We "cook the books" at Enron. In Japan, you "saba o yomu" (count the mackerel). In this country where a lot of food comes from the sea, fish are brought in all the time. As the mackerel are brought in and thrown from the ship into market boxes, the mackerel seem to fly by at high speed. They go so fast, it's hard to count. Turn that around – they go so fast, it's easy to *cheat* on the count.

In America, a "country bumpkin" has a closed mind and a narrow world view. In Japan, such a person is "I no naka no kawazu" (a frog at the bottom of a well). Not much of a world view from there, either.

But it's not all so foreign. We in the English speaking world have concluded, long ago, that "There is no medicine can cure an idiot." Half a world away, with no invaders sprinkling their language over the landscape, the Japanese, long ago, concluded the same thing. "Baka ni tsukeru kusuri wa nai" (To cure a fool there is no medicine can do it.).

No matter if you sing the praises of the Rising Sun or you sing the praises of the Rockets' Red Glare, the language reflects the human experience.

And that's the fun of toodling around through all these languages. Whether you're yodeling in German over the Alps or humming in a vineyard in Champagne; whether you're kvetching in Yiddish or convincing in Chinese or cajoling in Japanese; whether a poem breaks your heart in Italian or cracks you up in Spanish, language makes us human.

No matter the language, no matter the country, we'll tell the tale of villains drinking their paycheck and swindling their partners and cheating their wives. In a thousand different ways we'll spin a yarn of heroes conquering the mountains, swimming the seas, capturing the flag. And when you open your eyes and open your ears, and hear it and read it and say it in a few different languages, you've found a way to reach out and touch all peoples in all places and all times.

That is the magic of language.

Now let's go impress some people at a cocktail party.

Chapter 17

Payoff. Impressing People at a Cocktail Party

A tiny reminder of what's written at the beginning of this book.

The lode star of the language aficionado.

The prime directive.

The, if we may slip into French for a moment, "Raison d'etre" (reason for being):

"The purpose of all knowledge is to impress people at cocktail parties."

If getting a bunch of languages under our belts is going to impress people at cocktail parties (and it will), then let's get to a cocktail party!

Every hour of study, every drop of sweat, every lesson you grind through, is going to pay off in silver dollars when you pull those languages out of your mouth, smooth as silk.

"Who IS that person!"
"Amazing!"
"How is that possible!"

Picture the scene.

Other people will be trying to impress people with *trivial* things:

1. Three Jags in the driveway, one in the shop.
2. Trophy wives nipped, tucked, and Pilatesized to perfection.
3. Kids at Harvard.
4. Condos overlooking Central Park, Squaw Valley, or the Loire.

5. Portfolios busting their buttons with swag.
6. Wine cellars with humidity control and a live-in sommelier.
7. Lear jets on call.
8. Necklaces that could choke a rhino.

But you, dressed in "Goodwill chic", wearing a 12 dollar Timex, driving a '74 Buick Regal with 280,000 miles on it, will have something *they* do not.

Languages.

The air is filled with the clink of real silver hitting real Wedgewood china. Clothes swish as beautiful people slither past beautiful people, each eyeing the other up and down and wondering, "Who did *her* facelift?" Champagne corks pop, but in the muted way of moneyed ease. Nothing tawdry here.

It's a beautiful evening, and it's the Hamptons with the Spielberg, Paul Simon crowd. Or maybe it's a chilly, leaves-at-their-peak night in Sundance with Robert Redford and company. Or it's a penthouse in Manhattan, Bill Gates' guesthouse along Lake Washington, or a power broker's townhome in Georgetown.

A semi-circle of bejeweled, befurred, beRolexed people gather around someone talking about, is it *Latin*?

"Tell me, you should know, do you think you need to learn Latin first, if you're going to become such a master of languages as you are?" an investment banker with Goldman-Sachs asks.

At the epicenter of all this attention, a man, apparently a linguist of some sort, waves off the compliment.

"Oh, how droll, master of languages, me. I wouldn't say that, exactly."

A tuxedoed waiter goes by, tray in hand, some unspeakably expensive hors d'oeuvres on board.

"Say, you wouldn't happen to have some pigs-in-blankets back in the kitchen somewhere, would you?" the linguist asks.

"About the Latin" the investment banker presses.

"About the pigs-in-blankets?" the man sends the waiter off with a wave of his hand.

"Latin, yes, good question." His eyes scan the nearby bar. All these flutes and stemmed red wine glasses. Who do you have to talk to around here to get a can of Old Style?

"No. That is a myth. Latin *does* form a good foundation for learning other languages. All the *Romance* languages are so named because they are based on the language of *Rome*. So, yes, if you went through the epic struggle of learning Latin, you would have a good grounding for all the languages that derive from it – Spanish, French, Portuguese, Italian, Romanian, plus others. Indirectly, it prepares you for other European languages too. BUT! And this is the big BUT – why bother going through the trouble of learning a language that you can never use? Especially when you can use all that effort to learn a language you CAN use (say Spanish), which can ALSO serve as a foundation for the other languages."

A ripple of murmurs and approval. The investment banker nods. Surely, this man knows of what he speaks!

"But once you venture outside the Romance languages, that must be extra hard, is it not?" A woman in a black gown, a constellation of diamonds, and plucked-to-invisibility eyebrows asks.

The linguist at the center wonders if calling in a pizza from Domino's would be considered gauche, since he has yet to see a single foodstuff he recognizes.

"Well, I blush to disclose, it's outside the realm of the Romance languages that the linguist really earns his keep" he says. "Or her keep."

Oh, that's rich! The women gathered round break into a giggle at this rapier thrust of political-correctness wit. This John Stewart of the polyglot set is *too much*.

"Your best 'next language' is German. The grammar can be a little brutal, but it gives you a springboard into a bunch of related languages."

What's on *that* tray? At last, teriyaki chicken on a big toothpick. How to get that waiter over here. Is whistling allowed here? The linguist wonders.

"Such as?"

He's able to snag a teriyaki stick, grabs two more in case the great famine breaks out, and answers with mouth full and teriyaki juice dripping down on his Target-purchased white shirt.

"Gdgujch, schschweedisssssch, oops."

"Pardon?"

A slurp, a sleeve across the mouth, one big swallow, then, "Dutch, Swedish, all the Scandinavian languages. Anywhere they have real blondes."

That snaps back the head of more than one platinum head in the crowd.

"Now if you jump to Russian."

"Surely you don't speak that too?" one rapidly recovering blond head asks.

"Well…" Fact is, his command of the language is not particularly good. Shrugging it off at a cocktail party is one surefire way to create the opposite impression. God forbid someone comes along to test him. That's when you either beg off and go to the bathroom, or else you pull the fire alarm.

"But once you do have Russian down, then that opens up Polish and Serbo-Croatian, just in case you're of a mind to learn those as well", the linguist says, again, laying out the idea that he speaks these perfectly. Which he does not.

Maximum impact with minimal knowledge.

Cocktail party impressmanship at its acme and pitch.

"Someone said you speak Arabic too" a bearded, important looking man asks. (Maybe a producer? Writer? Somebody famous but whose face you don't see much.)

"Schwaya, schwaya" the linguist says. "That means a *little*, and I do mean a *little*."

Gales of laughter at that one. Nothing like a little self-put-down to tear them up.

"And those Oriental languages, howsoever did you master those?" yet another could-be-famous-but-doesn't-get-in-front-of-the-camera person asks.

Miracle of miracles, the waiter does come out of the kitchen with a whole tray of pigs-in-blankets. This *is* a good party after all.

"Say, you there, you!"

The waiter at the cocktail party pauses, tray of finger-food goodies in hand, and faces the man.

"Would you like one?" the waiter asks.

"Those are pigs-in-blankets, are they not?" the linguist asks. His fingers shine slick and shiny from the earlier encounter with the teriyaki sticks.

"Pigs-in-blankets? That they are indeed," the waiter answers, holding the tray out for the man's delectation.

"Looks like you've got a heavy burden there, compadre," the linguist says, "Permit me to succor you in your hour of need."

He tilts the tray towards his little plate, slides four of the little blanketed piggies onto the plate, uses one of the delicacies to shovel up a glop of stone-ground mustard onto his plate, and winks.

"Surely I must be hearing the flutter of angels' wings." The linguist pops a pig-in-blanket into his mouth, then over and around his now-stuffed face, he says, "Must have died en route to this here soirée. Got detoured to heaven. I'm given to understand it's *all* finger food in heaven."

"Now then, where were we?" the linguist asks the breathless circle of hangers-on. People hold their mini-quiches and baby cheesecake-laden plates at mid chest height with one hand, their champagne flutes or wine glasses with the other hand.

Enya music seeps through the party, loud enough to tickle the Celtic-loving nerve endings, but not so loud as to stopper conversation.

191

The linguist pounds down another pig-in-blanket. "I believe we were talking about the letter I wrote to my brother in Icelandic."

"No, we were talking about the Oriental languages," someone reminds.

"Oh yes," the man says, now using the pig-in-blanket to punctuate his points. "Brutal, that's all there is to it. Brutal, takes a lot of hard work. I found the only way I could get anywhere with the Chinese tone system was to go to a university, post a sign at the Student Union, and hire a private tutor. That did the trick."

"Amazing."

"Well," the pig-in-blanket went around in a little circle in the air, as if to say, "It was nothing."

"Oh, but do tell about the Icelandic!" One of the younger crowd jumps in. "How did you learn that?"

"Is that like Irish?" another man asks. "They're sort of close, aren't they? Ireland and Iceland?"

The man turns his head left and right, hoping there might be a globe or world map somewhere nearby.

A group geography-seek ripples through the dozen people gathered around the Icelandic letter-writing, pig-in-blanket eating man.

"Yeah, there's England, then Ireland, then Greenland, wait…"

"No, Iceland's before Greenland."

"Wait, where are the Shetlands? Aren't they up there?"

"And the Orkneys too, aren't they?"

"And the Faroes."

"What are the Faroes? I heard of the Shetlands."

"Are there Faroe ponies? There are *Shetland* ponies."

"Are there Iceland ponies?"

"What would they eat in Iceland?"

"I don't know, the same stuff they eat in Shetland, I guess."

"Maybe they just eat ice?"

The linguist slips away, temporarily unnoticed as the knot of people wrestles with Icelandic geography and pony feeding habits.

The linguist has served his purpose, has fulfilled his mission.

He has impressed people at a cocktail party. And he's scored some pigs-in-blankets. Life is good.

Gliding over to a clot of people by the bar, the man snags a spinach and cream cheese stuffed croissant-ette from another passing tray.

That damned croissant must have just come out of the oven. The cream cheese squishes out of one end and hits the man's tongue like magma fresh out of Kilauea.

"Aaaaa!", he snags a glass of wine out of a tall man's hand and pours it into his mouth. He distinctly feels the outline of his entire sinus system as cream cheese/wine steam scalds its way all the way up his nose.

"You OK?" the tall man asks.

The man nods, though his tongue has the distinct feel of sandpaper. Damn. The linguist won't be able to taste anything for a week, between the scalded taste buds and the steam-stripped nasal passages.

The linguist nods, wipes off his mouth, and gathers himself.

"Sorry about that inelegant entrance," he says, generating a round of smiles. "Let me regenerate that glass of wine for you."

"Oh, that's OK," the tall man says.

"Funny you should mention the Swahili language," the linguist says.

People look around. Swahili? I don't remember anyone saying anything about Swahili.

"It just so happens…"

Epilog

What Happened to Everybody?

So what happened to the cast of characters that danced across these pages?

Kim Gallagher, whose quote was taken for the foreword, is working for General Electric in Princeton, New Jersey. He's a big history buff and has visited nearby Revolutionary and Civil War battle sites.

None of the Russian sailors defected. The ship's doctor took the cookie but was never seen to eat it.

The French café owner, the Italian woman sweeping on her porch, the Portuguese woman on the beach? Unknown fates. We wish them well, one and all.

The student who "couldn't learn a foreign language" married the Italian woman and lives in Italy to this day.

The Madrid bed-and-breakfast woman did not get tetanus.

Maria Luisa had an uneventful recovery from her operation and was still smiling when the Interplast team left.

Polly the Parrot continues to amaze with her verbal acrobatics.

The Mozambique Olympic Team went home and who knows?

The doctor in the cellar full of wounded men survived imprisonment and returned to America after the war. His son was William B. Gallagher, his grandson Chris Gallagher.

The fellow traveler never got his *Teach Yourself Italian* book back from that Iowa woman.

The guy impressing everyone in the cocktail party in Chapter 17 never actually got *invited* to a cocktail party. So he hasn't had a chance to flash that polyglot savoir-faire yet.

He runs to the mailbox every day, looking for an invitation, any invitation, to a cocktail party. You can reach me through the publisher if, by chance, you should ever find yourself one guest short at YOUR next cocktail party.

The first author of this book never actually typed any of these words, but his language savvy inspired them. All the tips on how to learn *a* language, and how to learn *many* languages, come directly from him. His daughter penned his obituary just a short time ago.

> On June 15, 2007, "Dr. Bill" completed his last act on the stage of this life. He was 82 years old and ready to move on. He is very sadly missed by his children and grandchildren.
>
> While working as a general surgeon he also spent months at a time volunteering his service on the ship Hope in Peru, in a civilian hospital in Viet Nam during the war there, and on a Navajo Indian Reservation. In Tucson, he received the Volunteer Physician of the Year Award for his years of work with the Flying Samaritans – an all volunteer medical group who opened a free clinic in Mexico. We love you Dad – your "kiddos."

Through this, *his* book, he speaks to us still.

The authors wish to thank the following people:

Charles the Pharmacist at Tampa General Hospital. (Chinese)

The patients, doctors, and nurses at Bac Lieu Hospital in (then) South Vietnam, now Vietnam. (Vietnamese)

The patients, doctors, and nurses of Umea Sjukhuset in Umea, Sweden. (Swedish).

Patients in Minnesota, Wisconsin, Missouri, Georgia, North Carolina, California, Florida and New York. (Spanish, Creole, German, Polish, Russian, Japanese, Italian, French, you name it).

Resident doctors in Milwaukee and La Crosse, Wisconsin, who studied under William Gallagher. Resident doctors in Durham, North Carolina, Miami, Florida, and Stony Brook, New York, who studied under Chris. (Every language named in this book.)

Patients in Ecuador, on the ship HOPE, and in the clinics of the Flying Samaritans. (Spanish)

People on trains, planes, waiting rooms, restaurants, sidewalks. People on the beaten path and off it. Language teachers making recordings for Pimsleur and Rosetta Stone and every kind of language book. (Every language mentioned in this book.)

To 1,001 people who have put up with our garbled grammar, mistaken tones, and vocabulary mix-ups. Thanks for putting up with our efforts to speak your language.

To all of you, we say:

Gracias

Merci

Danke

Spaseeba

Domo domo

Tak

Dank U

Grazie

Xie xie

Obrigado

Thank you.